RIDING SUCCESS
WITHOUT STRESS

RIDING SUCCESS
WITHOUT STRESS

Joni Bentley

J.A. ALLEN
London

British Library Cataloguing in Publication Data
A catalogue record for this book is available from the British Library

ISBN 0-85131-701-4

Published in Great Britain in 1999 by
J.A. Allen and Company Limited,
4 Lower Grosvenor Place,
Buckingham Palace Road,
London SW1W 0EL

© Joni Bentley

Design by Nancy Lawrence
Typeset in Janson by Textype, Cambridge
Colour separation by Tenon & Polert Colour Scanning (HK) Ltd
Printed in Hong Kong by Dah Hua International Printing Press Co. Ltd.

CONTENTS

LIST OF ILLUSTRATIONS

All line illustrations by Su McGregor

LIST OF PHOTOGRAPHS

Photographs by Elizabeth Furth, except for Nos. 1, 15 reproduced by permission of The Society of Teachers of the Alexander Technique, Nos. 9, 10, 33, by Kersten Harris, and Nos. 14, 16 and 20, reproduced by permission of *Your Horse*.

PREFACE

The Alexander technique is a training system that teaches you to harness and maximise the full potential of your mind body/ functioning by raising your awareness. I want to emphasise that it is *not* a dressage training technique, unless it is taught by a qualified equestrian trainer who is also a qualified Alexander teacher. Unfortunately, this double qualification is quite rare.

I would also like to emphasise that the information on the Alexander technique given in this book should not be seen as a substitute for practical lessons in the technique. I would there-fore advise interested readers to seek out a *registered* Alexander teacher for lessons to put them on the right track. At this junc-ture I should add a word of warning.

Because the Alexander technique has had so much publicity in the horse world it has become very trendy, and some unscrupulous people are advertising themselves as offering the Alexander technique. What often happens is that they have been on a few Alexander workshops, after which they set them-selves up as teachers. Many use their local qualified Alexander teacher to draw you in – which is great in that you can learn a lot – but straight Alexander teachers usually know nothing about horses, and conflict arises when you are handed back to the person who advertised the riding lessons. At this juncture you are taught the same old routine, which often conflicts with your Alexander lessons. A certain person who had four lessons from me set herself up as an Alexander teacher in competition with me, telling the students that I had trained her. A little knowledge is a dangerous thing! People started to ring me up saying that they were having neck and back problems after their lessons and could I help them.

Another reason why these goings on are a cause for concern is that they are short-changing the potential of Alexander's great discovery; people are being put off before they realise its full potential. The Alexander teacher-training course is a three-year full time course and all qualified Alexander teachers are registered, so check up on them – there is a list of governing bodies at the back of this book. Because of incredible demand I have set up a *Riding Success Without Stress* practitioner-training course, which is a combination of the Alexander technique and the classical school (i.e. not a straight Alexander teacher-training course). If you would like a list of the teachers, or to know more about the course or workshops, please write to my mailing address at the back of this book.

FOREWORD

There is a lot of mystique and misinformation about the Alexander Technique in general and, in particular, in its application toward riding. Joni Bentley's book clarifies the application admirably. Being an experienced teacher in both disciplines, riding and the Alexander Technique, Ms. Bentley, therefore is a qualified guide to the area where the two disciples meet. She does this in such a practical and disarming way you one do not get intimidated. Yet I don't think anyone should underestimate the enormity of her message.

This book has many helpful photographs and illustrations but you won't find it filled with celebrity equestrians. This is obviously not an accident. One of the core themes can be seen in the chapter where she talks about the necessity to drop the ideal and take a more realistic approach. Before anyone gets the idea that she is advocating some kind of lowering of standards, they should read carefully. I don't think she is accepting just any principles. I think she is promoting very specific principles, which are, to my mind, very classic principles. Most of us probably look at a great rider as someone who literally embodies the set of universal riding principles and I think it is easy to assume we should copy this rider's body. Since no two of us are alike this is always a mistake. It is the principles housed inside a particular body form that we must develop. When we understand the universal principles and apply them to the reality of our own particular bodily limitations, we can succeed, as Ms. Bentley says. Here she is in some very strong company. Alexander himself, Gueriniere, and the great psychologist Jung all dislike imitation and warned of its pernicious dangers.

Joni Bentley's book is filled with interesting ways for a rider to learn to understand and feel these universal principles in the body they have now! Never does she present riding as unreachable and exclusive, on the contrary, her style is always encouraging, practical and inclusive.

Paul

Paul Belasik
Kennet Square, Pennsylvania USA

INTRODUCTION

The rider, the 'human genius' that refines random nature into an edifice, is the ultimate beneficiary of this art. Provided he understands his horses well, the rider will have created beauty that is the physical aesthetic manifestation of his intellectual understanding and spiritual depth. So can man be elevated by the taming of his horse, through a partnership with him, to become himself the object and the subject of his art.'

Charles De Kunffy

This quotation gives us a glimpse of how, in training our horses, we have the vehicle for our own self-development, irrespective of our level as a rider. We are lucky nowadays to have so many teaching tools at our disposal with which to develop self-mastery and success; tools that took past masters of what we now call 'mind management' whole lifetimes to discover. They discovered that it is by attending to the cultivation of one's own mind that we achieve genius and success in performance.

The tools included in this book result from the work of many masters who bequeathed us these gems with which to carry on where they left off. They all agreed that success begins with heightening our awareness of ourselves and how we react to the outside world. Thus the journey to success begins by working from inside to out.

In this book I will bring to your attention certain obstacles that sway us from the path of self-discovery, for example ego-centric personalities who profess to be classical trainers when they are not. I do this because their misguided concepts and influences are detrimental to your development and success. In some cases the classical principles have became so stretched and distorted by these personalities that love for the horse has been degraded to downright cruelty. The classical literature says, time and time again, that its training principles are based on love for the horse; on bringing out under saddle the grace and beauty a horse naturally displays at liberty. Yet we hear so many stories of horses being trussed up in draw reins; being abused with whip and spur – even being run into walls (some horses literally trying to crawl up them, away from their trainer/rider). Such horses (rather than the trainer or rider concerned) are then labelled bad or disobedient.

So what has happened, and how has training become so distorted? Bad teachers, lacking refinement and knowledge, excel in an ego-based society. They are usually successful because they will go to any lengths to win. They are very good at self-promotion and showing bravado to their followers, like the school bully attracting people who are not very established in their own selves. Because of their success in competition they gain high prestige and status in society. Unfortunately, their often undesirable methods are made available to the masses. Thus are the socially accepted standards set.

In *Misconceptions and Simple Truths in Dressage* Dr. H.L.M. Van Schaik writes:

> In 1893 W.J. Gordon wrote a book called *The Horse's World Of London*. I found therein an interesting concept which I quote: 'The ease with which a man will lose his eye for a horse is notorious. Let even a good judge live for a while among second-class horses and he will insensibly modify his ideal; and he will only get back to his true taste by another stay in first-class company.' It seems to me that this is also applicable to dressage judges; I wonder if any of the present-day judges have ever been exposed to real equestrian art, when the horse gave the impression of doing all the movements of his own accord and when 'the use of the rider's hand and legs were so secret that the eye could not catch them' (L'Hotte, *Questions Equestres*).

I pick up magazines, videos, books and go to shows, only to find stiff, browbeaten horses partnered by riders who are far from elegant in their positions and aids.

Why does society assume that, because someone is successful in competition, they can be a teacher of people. Most talented performers are good at teaching horses, but it is neither their field nor skill to teach people. The best teachers tend to be those who have failed, struggled and conquered like Alexander; through his own failure, not being able to perform because of throat problems, he helped others to succeed. People stifle their own learning and success by leaping on the ego bandwagon. It is so trendy to seek out a fashionable competitor turned trainer, but in the majority of cases their followers are only learning the art of imitation, and in many cases basking in the trainer's glory to put themselves up.

Superficial education leads to low standards and lack of vision. This realisation hit me very strongly one evening after giving a lecture/demonstration near London. An international eventer offered himself as my guinea-pig. Teaching him and his horse was a delight; they responded so easily. By the end of half an hour, horse and rider had transformed what was a feverish, crooked, choppy performance into one that floated above the ground with ease and grace. When we'd finished he was thrilled: 'It's amazing to learn how to straighten and calm a horse in such a logical, easy way – and quite frankly I'm shocked at how big my horse's paces are.' I told him he had given the audience a good opportunity to see the importance of sound basic training, before beginning lateral work.

'Don't expect these riders to see the improvement; they struggle to see if a horse is sound. People often turn up for lessons with me on lame horses – if they can't see that how do you expect them to see the difference between a floating and a mechanical action', he said.

Later feedback confirmed his words: 'It's above their heads', another trainer said. If these simple, basic principles are above people's heads what on earth are they learning? I think it's so sad that, because of a lack of awareness in our education system, riders get stuck at such a novice level. The reason for the failure is not the pupils but the great, gaping holes in the basic training of horse and rider. I find it very sad that, so often, the kindly novice's aspirations are held back by 'almighty' teachers who actively discourage their students from thinking for themselves.

Everybody is unique and special in what they have to offer. A good teacher will bring that out of their student. With correct training and personality building, this superficiality drops away, restoring the visions of the classical masters. This book is written to open the eyes of students who really want to see; to be able to discriminate between good trainers and bad ones; to avoid putting both their own and their horse's lives in the wrong hands. The book will show you that teacher is *not* always right, and will help you to trust your own gut feelings more, before all the doubts in your head start interfering.

This book is also designed to help riders to become more process- rather than outcome-directed. That means that they will use the means to justify the end, rather than the opposite – the end justifying the means, at any cost. Cast iron rules lead to impersonal teaching, but horses and riders are all unique individuals, with personal needs and difficulties. Successful businessmen will always tell you that if you look after the pennies, the pounds look after themselves. In the same way, if you look after the means, the end will look after itself, and success is guaranteed.

I hope that through reading this book, you will come to find the teacher inside yourself, helped by your horse's precious feedback and patience. Journeying in this way will not only be illuminating, but you will also achieve the success you and your horse deserve in a far shorter time than you ever imagined.

PART ONE

EARLY BEGINNINGS

As in most athletic endeavors, the rider must develop the
seemingly contradictory qualities of relaxation and strength.
Relaxation allows horse and rider to harmonize, not only by
virtue of absence of discomfort or pain, but by finding pleasure
in moving through space in cooperative unity.

Charles de Kunffy

CHAPTER 1

Whilst training to be a teacher of the Alexander technique I
began to realise that there are remarkable parallels in training
horses and humans towards their full potential. Horses and riders exhibit similar reflex responses which, I suppose, is not sur-
prising since they are both vertebrates – albeit one organised
horizontally and the other organised vertically (see Figure 1).

While I was undergoing my three-year Alexander teacher
training course, I was amazed how the principles of classical
dressage and Frederick Matthias Alexander's discovery mirrored
each other. The techniques are so similiar and interchangeable.
By combining the two worlds, riding could now achieve even
greater heights through applying this much – needed dimension
– classical human training. So many students attending my
courses for the first time complained that their trainer always
focused too much on the horse, leaving them to feel as though
they were hindering rather than helping the horse's process.
As I watched them ride I had to admit they were right. The
horse only mirrors the rider and, if there is a problem, it is the
rider's responsibility not the horse's. By applying my own
knowledge to their requests, the concept of *Riding Success
Without Stress* was born.

For very many years we have been blessed with the knowledge of the great masters of classical dressage. Now we can

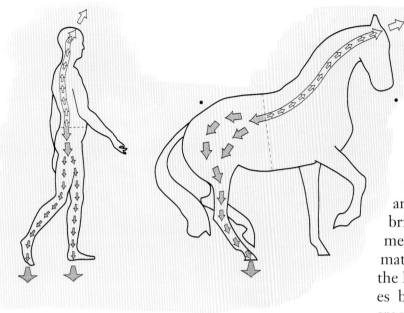

Figure 1   Comparative reflex responses of horse and rider.

equal the partnership up by adding to it the Alexander Technique.

Before the Alexander technique was developed, what was considered to be good posture left a lot to be desired. Shoulders back, stomach in; head back stiff as a ramrod, clearly unsuitable for riders to absorb the movement of any horse. The Alexander technique brings more brilliance, ease of movement and grace to riding and it is only a matter of time before it shines through the horse world. After all, how can horses be calm, straight and forward with crooked and tense riders?

Using the Alexander technique riders will learn how to develop collection and self-carriage in their own bodies, aiding the horse rather than hindering him; adding more brilliance and power to their joint performance. Without collection in the rider the horse tends to become heavy on the forehand, leaning on the rider's hand, developing a hard, damaged mouth and trailing quarters. This scenario leads eventually to back problems, hence the need for so many back practitioners these days. When the rider is straight and in self-carriage, the horse uses that support to improve the way he carries himself. A good rider *holds* the horse with the seat – a concept not to be confused with the driving, pushing or pulling that is unfortunately so prevalent today.

Escaping from Barbarism

So often I find Advanced dressage horses struggling to contort their bodies in order to achieve the advanced movements demanded by the rider, without the foundation of lowered, engaged quarters that any training worth its salt builds first.

The consequent strain often causes damaged, deformed sacrum, stifles, hocks and fetlocks.

If the horse received the benefit of much-needed knowledge, elevation and engagement of the rider's seat (head, neck, back and legs) would be used to elevate the forehand and free the horse's shoulders, neck and poll. Insensitive, even brutal, trick riding and a hit and miss approach would then become things of the past, and all the gadgets flooding the market would remain on the shelf where they belong.

Over two thousand years ago, Xenophon pointed out that reliance on 'quick-fix' training methods short-circuits the learning process and aborts the birth of a real understanding between horse and rider:

> Anything forced or misunderstood can never be beautiful. If a dancer were forced to dance by whip or spikes he would be no more beautiful than a horse trained under similar circumstances. What a horse does under compulsion he does blindly . . . The performances of horse or man so treated are displays of clumsy gestures rather than of grace and beauty. What we need is that the horse should of his own accord exhibit his finest airs and paces at set signals . . . Such are the horses on which gods and heroes ride.

Yet still we are using force and constraint in training horses. How far have we really progressed in our philosophy of horsemanship? At horse shows it's more common to see stiff, frightened, angry horses and riders rather than partnerships of harmony and grace associated with 'gods and heroes'. 'Caring' techniques are often considered 'off the wall' or 'soft' but many examples from classical equestrian literature will show that they are not new – they have simply been forgotten as a result of man's misguided modern-day greed. Charles De Kunffy, in *Training Strategies For Dressage Riders*, makes the point concisely:

> Classical horsemanship is based on love for the horse, it is not practised for the glorification of the rider . . . We must make a choice between self love, the promotion or the well-being of our own ego, and love of the horse. That is the fundamental attitudinal decision that earned Xenophon the title Father of Classical Dressage: he dared to love a horse!

> 'We shall take great care not to annoy the horse and spoil his friendly charm, for it is like the scent of a blossom – once lost it will never return.'
>
> de Pluvinel

Since Xenophon was a Greek general, I doubt that he would qualify as a 'softie'.

We have now reached a time when we have refined training tools at our disposal. It is time to wake up and drop the hard, fear-based, barbaric attitudes that abound in the horse world: 'You've got to be the boss and beat him into submission'; 'Horses are stupid', etc. Horses are not machines; they live, breathe and feel, and they are incredible sensitive, noble creatures, who love to be care-takers and to please their masters, unless they are abused and bent out of shape by man.

Now armed with the knowledge of the Alexander technique, let us move forward and go deeper into learning, enjoying an understanding of how mind, body and spirit of horse and rider work together as a whole whilst performing their art. High school movements produced in dressage originate from the movements made naturally by a horse displaying high spirits and joie de vivre. Opening to spirit must be the foremost consideration when training horses. Horses have feelings that must be honoured. Here are de Pluvinel's great words of advice:

'We shall take great care not to annoy the horse and spoil his friendly charm, for it is like the scent of a blossom – once lost it will never return.'

Training Essentials

As a trainer, it is important to me that the knowledge imparted has certain attributes. It must be:

Traditional. The training techniques are steeped in tradition and have stood the test of time, thus making them reliable.

Holistic. Whilst remaining simple and constructive, it must take into account the relationship of mind, body and spirit of both horse and rider.

Well structured. The knowledge must be structured and given in such a way that the student can build on it, working clearly and correctly in the absence of the teacher. In this way students begin to 'own' their own training system and partnership with their horse. They progress rather than decline between lessons.

Disciplined. Discipline must be built into the rider because success in any form of learning depends on raising awareness of one's own mind and body functioning to their optimum.

When the head, neck and back of both horse and rider are restricted – and most are – the free flow of energy that gives the lift for elevation is blocked, resulting in pain and tension throughout their bodies and laboured, mechanical movements. Therefore, just as Alexander was concerned with good human posture, I am concerned about the horse's posture, especially at higher levels of dressage where the movements are so demanding that if they are performed biomechanically incorrectly, they will damage the horse. Thus more emphasis must be put on the quality of the horse's carriage in his paces than on where he puts his feet!

CHAPTER 2

ALEXANDER'S WISDOM

What a piece of work is man! how noble in reason! how infinite in faculty in form and moving how expressed and admirable! in action how like an angel! in apprehension how like a god! the beauty of the world! the paragon of animals!

Shakespeare

As a young man over one hundred years ago, Frederick Matthias Alexander was inspired by these lines of Shakespeare's. However when he later discovered how much we 'misuse' ourselves in daily life, how unreliable our sensory appreciation is, and how ruled we are by our conditioned response, he said:

> For what could be less 'noble in reason', less 'infinite in faculty' than that man, despite his potentialities, should have fallen into such error in the way he uses himself and in this way brought about such a lowering in his standards of functioning that in everything he attempts to accomplish, these harmful conditions tend to become more and more exaggerated?

Strong words, but as you read through this book you will see the truth in them.

If we learn to function in life with good use of mind and body, we increase our potential for succeeding in riding. We will view it in a more creative way, see it as more challenging, and be more likely to achieve our goals. Alexander's teaching offers you your birthright to return to Shakespeare's vision and enrich all areas of your life.

Photo 1
Frederick Matthias Alexander.

The Man and His Discovery

Before discussing Alexander's technique and its applications to riding in more detail, I would like to acquaint you with the man himself, and outline the circumstances which led to his discovery.

Alexander was born on 20 January 1869 at Wynyard, a small town in north-west Tasmania. He was the eldest of eight children.

A weak and sickly child, although very precocious, he was privately coached by the village schoomaster. He spent much of his time out of doors observing animal life and nature in the virgin country around his home and in swimming, boating and fishing. As his health improved, from the age of eight or nine onwards, he devoted himself to horses; his love of them and his expert knowledge of their training and management remained with him all his life.

In 1885, at the age of sixteen, Alexander began work as a clerk with a nearby tin mining company, and studied accountancy in his spare time. However, from early childhood he had been interested in acting, elocution and dramatic recitals which, in those days, were the principal form of entertainment both publicly and at private social functions. He had already shown considerable natural aptitude both as a performer and a producer of amateur theatricals and, within three years, he had saved enough money to go to Melbourne for professional training.

In Melbourne he lived with an uncle and aunt while he took lessons in elocution, dramatic art and the violin from the best teachers. He also paid frequent visits to theatres, concerts, and art galleries, and formed his own amateur dramatic company. When his funds ran out, he took clerical and accountancy jobs, and also worked as a tea-taster, but with a recurrence of his early illness, his dislike of commercial life and his (at the time) violent temper, he did not hold many of them for long. However, he had now decided to make his career as a professional elocutionist and reciter, and once again saved enough money for training and for a few months rest and recuperation.

Through his production of plays, his recitals, concerts and private engagements, Alexander was becoming well-known and, at the age of twenty-five, he decided to return home and try a professional three-month tour of Tasmania. His mother gave him full support in his choice of career, but his father was distressed that his eldest son should have become 'a strolling player and a vagabond'. He performed in Wynyard, Waratah, Launceston and Hobart with great success, and made arrangements through friends to open a tour in New Zealand early in 1894.

Critics in Melbourne and Tasmania had given Alexander good notices, and his reception in New Zealand was already assured. He had occasional brushes with individuals who took exception to his forthright manner of approaching problems, but generally he made friends very easily, and professional colleagues and influential people in the towns he visited went out of their way to befriend and help him. What no one could do anything about, however, was an increasing tendency for his throat to fail him towards the end of his recitals, no matter how much he rested it before such occasions, as several doctors had advised. Nevertheless, he continued his tour with five weeks in Christchurch, six weeks in Wellington, a month in Napier and six months in Auckland.

For some time, Alexander had been watching himself closely in the mirror, trying to find out experimentally what it was that he did with himself which, he was convinced, led to his voice failing in recital. He was also carefully studying breathing methods and voice production, because it had been pointed out to him that he was beginning to gasp for air at the end of a sentence. Diaphragmatic and costal breathing was then the fashion, but Alexander tried and rejected this, and began to evolve his own method.

The farmer sows seeds with faith in Existence, losing the seeds he holds in his hand and gaining much more.

P. R. Shankar

This, while not fully evolved, was already sufficiently revolutionary to attract much attention, especially among the amateurs in his audience who heard him recite. A number of them approached him privately to seek his help, and although he had never considered the possibility of teaching, he announced on the last night of his series of recitals in Auckland, his intention to give lessons in voice production and breathing. Within a few weeks he was taking pupils from nine o'clock in the morning until ten or eleven at night.

After three months, he decided, because of family commitments, that he would teach in Australia (turning down offers to go to America and elsewhere). Before he sailed, he gave a farewell performance in Auckland, where a packed audience of pupils and the general public presented him with a hand-illuminated testimonal of appreciation, the signatures being headed by that of the Mayor of Auckland.

Years later, speaking of the development of his technique, Alexander said: 'It was in Auckland during those last three months that I got the idea of what it really was – and could be'. Although he had realised so early on that what he had to teach had a far wider significance than mere voice training, his friends in Melbourne, where he took teaching rooms, were at a loss to

The horse's head should hang like a chandelier from a free – floating neck and spine.

understand what he hoped to achieve. However, after a few weeks of teaching singers and other performing artists, Alexander received for lessons a local doctor's son, who was suffering from pulmonary tuberculosis. Shortly afterwards, the same doctor sent a woman patient with adhesions of the lungs. Another doctor, learning of the improvements that Alexander brought about in these pupils, sent him a girl with spinal trouble. Soon, the number of pupils who had been introduced as patients by their doctors exceeded the number of stage and theatrical personnel he was teaching. A theological college, on medical advice, asked Alexander to teach a group of nineteen students primarily for voice production, but as with his other pupils now, they were taught first the 'use of the self'. The use of the voice and manner of breathing followed as a part of this teaching. Doctors and professors of the medical faculty at Melbourne University were also among Alexander's pupils and, after two years in Melbourne, he found himself well established with a wide range of pupils – both those who could be described as 'normal', and those who had been diagnosed by doctors as suffering from some specific complaint.

After three more years, Alexander's brother, A.R. Alexander, joined him as a teacher and he transferred his practice to Sydney. His reputation preceded him, and once again he was soon inundated with work. Dr J.W. Steward McKay, a famous surgeon practising at Lewisham Hospital in London, gave Alexander particular encouragement when he found that his technique was of great value in gynaecological cases, frequently overcoming the necessity for an operation on a patient. It was Dr McKay who, by his interest and understanding, confirmed Alexander in his belief that he had discovered something of a universal nature of great value to man; and it was he who persuaded Alexander to move to London in order to secure for his work the recognition that it merited.

Alexander sailed for London on 13 April 1904. For six years he lived and taught at rooms in the Army and Navy Mansions, Victoria Street, before moving to 16 Ashley Place, London SW1. Because of pressure of work, Alexander had to bring in both his brother and a sister to help with his ever-growing number of pupils. It also became necessary to attempt to put the principles of his work into print in order to forestall some would-be plagiarists who were jealous of his success. His book *Man's Supreme Inheritance* was eventually ready and constant demand kept it in print throughout the subsequent forty-five years of his life.

The First World War led to an immediate falling off in the number of pupils, and Alexander decided to go to America. Before the end of September 1914 he had more pupils than he could handle. Every year from 1914 to 1924 he crossed the Atlantic westwards around October and returned home to Britain in the spring. His second important book *Constructive Conscious Control of the Individual* was published in 1923.

During the early 1930s, a number of doctors in Britain began to take a special interest in Alexander's work and, with their enthusiastic support, some impression was made on the body of conventional medicine in Britain through discussion, lecture-debates and correspondence in the medical press.

In September 1930, a training course for student teachers was started at Ashley Place and, from that time until Alexander's death (except for the war years), there were always a number of people taking the three-year course which, if they had the capability, entitled them to set up in practice on their own as certificated Alexander teachers. This tradition has been continued ever since.

At the end of 1947, Alexander had a fall which displaced one rib and bruised several others. Within a week of this accident he suffered a severe stroke, losing the use of his left hand and leg, and experiencing paralysis of the side of his face. It is not often that a man of seventy-nine recovers from such an affliction, and the three doctors who attended him had little hope for Alexander. Yet, by March 1948, he was teaching again. In January 1949, his eightieth birthday was celebrated with a public dinner given in his honour at Brown's Hotel; Sir Stafford Cripps, then Chancellor of the Exchequer, took the chair. From then on Alexander continued to work actively, taking private pupils and supervising the work of his assistant teachers until 1955 when, after a chill and brief illness, he died suddenly on 19 October in his eighty-seventh year.

The information in this section was provided by Alexander's pupil, Walter Carrington.

THE PRIMARY FREEDOM

A soft but effective seat is dependent on the correct position of the rider's spine. On the one hand it must be supple enough to absorb the movement of the horse. On the other hand it must maintain sufficient stability to transmit the rider's aids effectively . . . The rider's spine gives firmness to his seat and also acts as a 'central control' from which all aids are transmitted and all the horse's reactions are received.

The Principles of Riding, the official instruction handbook of the German National Equestrian Federation

The Primary Control

The 'central control' the Germans are referring to is directly comparable to what Alexander calls the 'primary control'. So how easy is it to control this central control?

In his book *Thinking Allowed*, Alexander's pupil, Walter Carrington says: 'The relationship between the head and the body is very complex . . . Alexander was perfectly right in . . . saying that the primary control is a "certain relationship" of the head and neck and the body. A "certain relationship" is really the best you can say about it in words.' The point he is making is that, because the Alexander technique deals with actual biomechanical experiences, attempts to define them in abstract, in simplified terms, may fail to do them justice. It is rather like trying to describe a sunset to someone who cannot see it: your description may not be inaccurate, but it will be inadequate. However, Walter Carrington's wife, Dilys, in her pamphlet *Human Movement*, makes some very helpful observations on the topic:

Consider how a four-legged animal moves: the head is in front and the weight of the head is always being pulled downwards by the force of gravity – the head being held in the correct relationship for that animal by the necessary tone in the neck muscles. When the animal moves, its direction is usually forward, as the intention is to get the mouth or the nose or the eyes nearer something. The forward movement of the head exerts a slight forward pull on the spine. As the head moves forward leading the forward movement of the body the muscles controlling the back legs are activated and the hind legs step underneath the animal. (This is well understood by horsemen.) So as the animal moves, the spine is constantly being stretched, or as you might say, 'lengthened', but the movement begins at the head with the neck being 'freed' – i.e. as the neck muscles are released the head falls a fraction, pulled by gravity, and is then directed along the line of the spine.

The basic mechanisms are the same in Man. It is necessary for the centre of gravity of the head to be forward of the condyles of the skull – the joint between the head and neck – as that allows the head to fall slightly forward through the pull of the force of gravity when the neck muscles are released, thus overcoming inertia in beginning a movement. (This gives the 'forward' part of the direction 'forward and up'.) At the same time the head has to be directed 'upwards' to keep the stretch along the length of the spine that the animal gets easily by moving forward. The movement of the legs in walking, with the forward direction of the knees, gives the two-way stretch on the spine in the same way as in the animal . . .

Just as a well-balanced animal moves by using gravity (drop of head) to overcome inertia, and at the same time uses its muscles to overcome the pull of gravity, letting them retain the desired length, rather than tighten unnecessarily so, in a well-balanced man, the head (with the centre of gravity forward of the condyles) tends to fall forward, whilst the urge to be upright causes the head to be directed upward along the length of the spine. The F.M. Alexander Technique is concerned with correcting balance and encouraging the anti-gravity mechanism of the body. As most children are born and begin their lives with the balance and movement mechanism working well, the brain knows the way the movement should take place. The Alexander teacher has primarily to help the pupil to stop (inhibit) his usual quick response to a stimulus, to take time to decide how he wants to react and then guide his movements, keeping the balance and the anti-gravity mechanism of the body at its optimum for the conditions of the pupil.

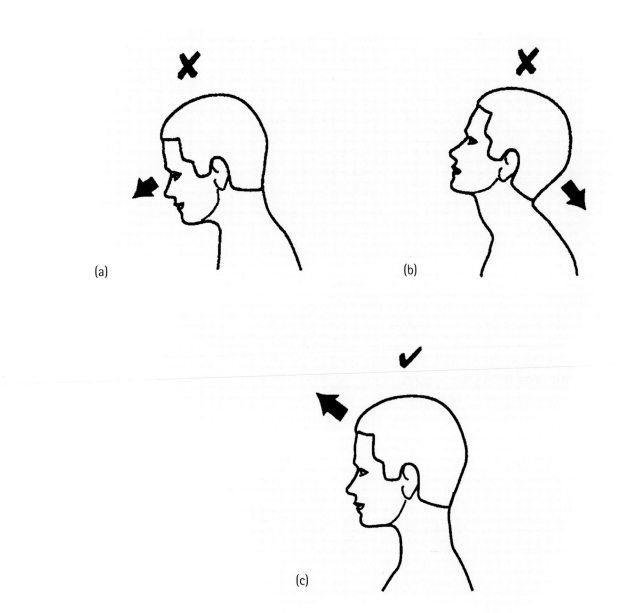

Figure 2   In Alexander terms, the head must be going forward and up leading the body in any movement, so that the body remains in balance using no more muscular tension than is necessary, like an animal: (a) forwards and down; (b) back and down; (c) forwards and up, leading the movement of the body.

Exploring Your Body's Balance in the Saddle

While you are sitting on a chair or saddle, the first thing I would like you to notice is how much energy you are using to sit. Are you sitting with too much energy, lifting yourself up off the chair? Or with too little energy, sitting down heavily into it?

Secondly, in order to sit in a classical position – for your upper body, head, neck and back to be balanced with ease and poise – you must sit on the lowest central point of your seat bones. My students say it helps to think of their seat bones as little feet ('seat feet') that are supporting the weight of the upper body and at the same time are opening up to the support of the horse/chair.

The seat bones are shaped like little rockers with a front, middle and back. To find the lowest central part, sit on your hands, palms upward. If you have difficulty finding the seat bones, rock from side to side until you can feel them. When you have found them, balance yourself on the lowest central part of their arc and distribute your weight evenly between them.

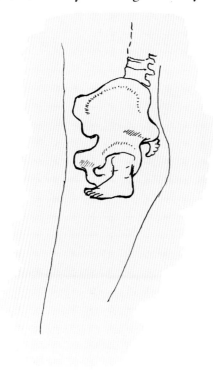

Figure 3
Riding 'in the movement': rider
balanced between the ball and
heel of the 'seat feet'.

As you are sitting on your hands, take your attention to the skin on the back of your hands. Notice how the weight of your upper body presses down into your hands then through them into the saddle/chair. Release the skin on the back of your hands more and invite the upward support of the horse/chair to come up into your seat bones – then into your pelvis, hips, waist, rib-cage, shoulders, neck, head – into the hollow in the roof of your mouth – into the dome at the top of your skull – through the scalp and forwards and up out into the world.

Do you feel any brighter? Open up your senses. Look around you and take in all the colours, textures, sounds, smells and other sensations.

Are you allowing enough support up to counterbalance the weight going down? The two exercises which follow will help you to experiment more.

Photo 2   Riding behind the movement.   Photo 3   Riding in front of the movement.

Exercise: riding behind the movement

To experiment with this more, rock very slowly backwards along the rim of the seat bones until you find the back edge (Figure 4) – you may have to lean back a long way. You will now be sitting with your pelvis tipped backwards. Notice how it has affected your head, neck, back, chest and shoulders. Do you feel any upward support from the chair/saddle beneath you, or are you pressing down too heavily to sense it? Come to the vertical again and try the next exercise.

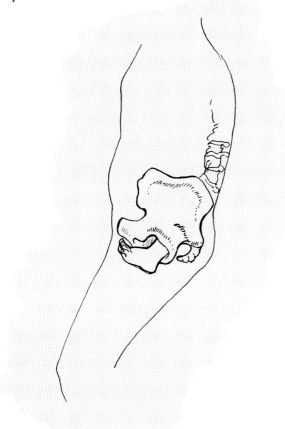

Figure 4
Rock slowly backwards along the rim of your seat bones until you find the back edge. Sitting like this keeps you riding behind the movement.

Exercise: riding in front of the movement

Now explore the front edge of the rockers. As you roll forwards, you will find that your lower back tends to arch and your rib-cage lifts (Figure 5). Rock back to the vertical position then to the front several times and notice how you come up and off your seat bones and they point out behind you.

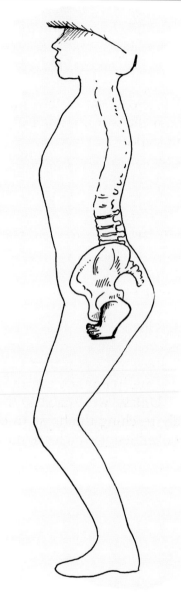

Figure 5   Rock to the front of your seat bones and notice how you come up and off them, hollowing your lower back, causing compression and making it impossible to absorb the horse's movement.

The purpose of rocking backwards and forwards is to find the lowest, most central part of the seat bones, which you need to sit on to be supported and in balance.

The Eyes

Alexander had very strong views about not fixing your gaze and thus shutting out the world around you. Having your eyes open helps you to balance. To test this, stand on one leg: you'll notice a lot of movement in the lower leg and foot. Now shut your eyes. Things are more difficult. Keep them shut and when you begin to feel that you are losing your balance open them quickly – is it easier to steady yourself with your eyes open?

Riders often withdraw their attention from the world, staring blankly at the floor – usually to the inside of a circle. You go where your attention goes, so if it goes down and into the inside of the circle, you can bet your bottom dollar you are tipping the horse in.

Establishing the primary control in the rider distributes their weight evenly over the horse's back and produces a deep but light seat that follows the movement of the horse's back without hindrance – and only then can the horse have a hope of being straight. Unless we establish this freedom in the rider we are merely teaching the horse to compensate for our bad habits and crookedness – which are the subject of the next chapter.

CHAPTER 4

DOES RIGHT FEEL RIGHT?

A wise man once said: 'The world is as we are.' Put another way
'A crooked man will walk a crooked mile.'

We are led to believe that our feelings are reliable, but could it be that we are wrong? We regard the distortion of our bodies, built up over long years, as normal, because we have forgotten what is really normal. For example, a young girl whose posture gave cause for concern was taken to Alexander for a lesson. Afterwards she ran to her mother and said 'Mummy, mummy, that man has pulled me all out of shape.' In fact, Alexander had pulled her into the right shape and she just didn't realise it. It didn't feel right; it wasn't what she was used to. What happens in such cases is that the feedback from our senses becomes unreliable; our perception is skewed.

Here is a description of one of my student's experiences of how right began to feel right:

On the wooden horse, although I felt straight, Joni immediately noticed that I was sitting too far to the right. My left knee and thigh were higher and more jammed against the saddle, and my left foot stuck out. Then Joni helped me to release my stiff right hip which was pulling my seat off to the right. She says this is a very common problem amongst riders and it causes crookedness in the horse's back. It was quiet alarming: I must say I felt incredibly unsafe and that I was hanging off so far to the left that I felt I would fall off any minute. I could have sworn she had had too many the night before!

On further investigation, she saw that I was also sitting too much on my fork, raising my chest and arching my lower back. I suspected there must be some truth in this because I held so much pain in it. With Joni's help I found the correct part of my seat bones, the deepest central lowest spot. Relaxing my chest into a more normal position released the ache in my lower back. But this felt so wrong. I had spent years building my position and now I felt like the proverbial 'sack of spuds'. Joni got me to look in the mirror to reassure me that it didn't look as bad as it felt. I couldn't believe how unreliable my feelings were. My position looked great! How could it feel so wrong and be so right?

Now, at last, I have the understanding of what a deep seat is. While riding I had been alternating between sitting on my fork and hiking my chest up and collapsing, tipping my pelvis back and driving my seat bones down into the horse's back, thinking that this was a deep seat – no wonder my horse gritted his teeth. My previous teachers had told me that this driving seat pushes the horse's hind legs under him and engages his quarters. As Joni continued working with me on the wooden horse the cramped up muscles caused by driving and hiking started to release and I felt a burning sensation between my shoulder blades – how knotted up I had become! As my back straightened up and released more, my legs seemed to grow out of my hip sockets until I had to drop my stirrups three holes.

Photo 4   Sitting too far to the right.

Figure 6   The faulty 'driving' seat. Rather than pushing the horse's hind
legs underneath him, this damages his back.

Acquired Crookedness

As a result of past tradition the majority of people today tend to be right-handed. This affects the right side of the body in that it makes it stronger but less flexible than the left. You can see in classrooms that children start from a very early age to curl around their writing hand, hiding their work by pulling their right shoulder down and round, compressing their right ribs, hiking up the right hip. This becomes a set crookedness which is then taken onto the horse. The rider sits pulled down to the right with the hips displaced to the left, creating a twist throughout their whole body (see Figure 7). Obviously, this affects the horse's way of going.

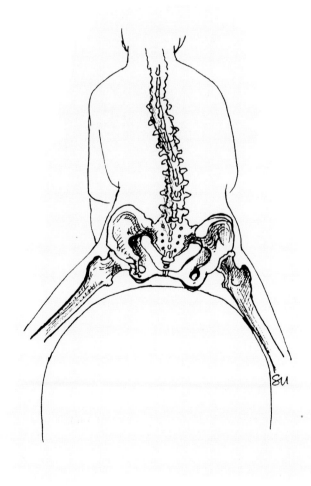

Figure 7
Acquired crookedness – rider
'leaking out' to the right, creating
twist throughout the whole body.

I remember watching a world-class rider/trainer teaching a Grand Prix rider. It was quite obvious to me that the rider was sitting too far to the right, which had resulted in twisting and dropping the horse's barrel down on that side (See Figure 7). The trainer, alarmed that a horse working at such a high level was doing so with his quarters trailing out miles behind, decided to work with piaffe to passage in the hope of creating some engagement. Both horse and rider looked stressed. On the right rein the uneven loading of the hind legs was, I would say, 75 per cent on the right and 25 per cent on the left. This unlevel action was putting the right hock under considerable strain, which showed up in its short, stiff action. The trainer activated the 'lazy' right hock with the whip. The horse grunted as he held his breath, obediently obliging – and the vicious circle continued.

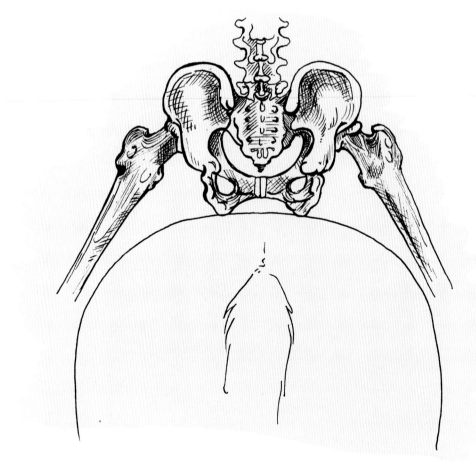

Figure 8   Sitting straight.

Developing Suppleness

In *Reflections On Equestrian Art*, Nuno Oliveira said:

> A good piece of advice to all who want to ride well, and who wish
> to acquire a good position, would be to do gymnastic exercises,
> which give suppleness, ease and sureness in riding . . . Only the
> rider who is free from any contraction will have a horse equally free
> from contraction. A team such as this is the ideal.'

The following exercise will help you to become supple, and
release some of your contractions. You will learn more about
your body, release your 'set' side and increase suppleness, which
will allow you to be more 'equal on both reins'.

Photo 5

Exercise: suppling and releasing
Sit in front of a mirror. Stretch your hands into
the air, fingertips pointing to the sky, palms
facing inwards (see Photo 5). Let the accumu-
lated weight of your head, then your neck,
followed by your shoulders, arms and the whole
of your upper body pass directly downwards
through your torso to the central lowest part of
your seat bones, until the weight is even. Notice
whether you have a tendency to lift
your chest or shoulders. If so, allow them to
release down, and notice whether tension
decreases in your lower back. Experiment also
by moving your head around, leading with
your eyes, and notice any effect this has on your
seat bones.

Next, just put up your right arm with fingertips pointing to the sky (Photo 6), and imagine
that on the end of each finger of your right
hand you have little strings that gently ease
your hand and arm and ribs up to the ceiling
and beyond. Hang from the 'strings'. Keep
your neck muscles released and your head

Photo 6

releasing up to the sky by continually growing upward through your fingers. Free your waist, and allow your right seat bone, hip and leg to fall down in the opposite direction by releasing your ribs. Now relax your right arm and repeat with the left.

Was there any difference between the right and left sides of your torso? If so, put both arms up together and allow the 'strings' to pull your arms up alternately, keeping your shoulders relaxed (Photos 7 and 8). Really allow your tight side to hang down and release from the 'strings' into the upward support of the chair. This will create an opposing stretch. Sense your weight changing as it passes down to your seat bones. The more you stretch up and allow your ribs to open and stretch, giving them life and space, the more you allow your lower body and seat bones to release down and receive the upward support of the chair. Use this exercise until you are equally supple in your right and left rib-cage – 'equal on both reins'. Your head should be moving in an upward direction – not tipping sideways – to keep you straight.

Photo 7   Photo 8

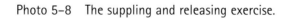

Photo 5–8   The suppling and releasing exercise.

At this point, I really recommend that you visit a registered Alexander teacher to keep you on the right track (see list of governing bodies at the end of this book).

CHAPTER

5

THE HYPNOSIS OF SOCIAL CONDITIONING

Guard the mind from the dust which flies in from the world.

P. R. Shankar

Children have good natural use of their bodies but, living in our complex and competitive society, this starts to decline after about the age of two. They begin to adapt to the 'hypnosis of social conditioning' that the world seems to be under.

Photo 9–10
Young child showing good natural use of the body.

Naturalness and grace decline over the years as all the tensions, pressure and stress build up in our nervous system.

Man's crackling ambition 'hits' our horses, raising a dichotomy because the whole point of dressage is to captivate those moments of joie de vivre that pulse through the horse's veins as he floats effortlessly, full of pride and joy across the field, exhibiting his grace, charm and beauty. How does that image fit into our competitive world today? In *Exploring Dressage Technique*, Paul Belasik writes:

> Classical riding is an artistic homage to nature . . . I myself hit a certain wall, focusing only on the technical plane . . . here many riders go astray. They use the discipline [monotonous technical exercises] as punishment for their apparent failures in achievement the same way they use a prize for reward. 'I only got the second prize. I have to work harder, drive myself and my horse harder.' 'My practice isn't good enough yet.' Pain becomes the big feeling as the work crackles with ambition.

Transactional Analysis

'Ignorance is bliss' so they say – but for whom? Transactional analysis was developed as a form of psychotherapy which enables people to see themselves more clearly so that they can change what they want to change and strengthen what they want to strengthen. According to transactional analysis theory, after birth we unconsciously learn how to cope with living in the world; it is the best way we can get love, attention and acceptance. We are conditioned by our parents' needs and they by their parents, and so on. In transactional analysis theory this is known as archaic parent conditioning. We each spend our life trying to live up to what our parents expect of us, generation after generation. For example, in her book, *My Mother, My Self*, Nancy Friday tells this story:

> A young woman had recently married. One day, she was cooking a leg of lamb. Before she put it in the oven, she cut the bottom of the leg off and then put the two pieces side by side in the roasting pan.
>
> 'Why do you do that?' asked her husband.

'I don't know, that's what my mother always does', she replied.

The husband then asked his mother-in-law why she chopped the bottom off her leg of lamb before cooking it.

'I don't know. That's what my mother always does', replied the mother-in-law. The grandmother was still alive, and there to tell the tale. When the young man asked her why she cut the bottom off her leg of lamb she told him: 'Because my roasting pan is very small, and it won't fit in otherwise'.

According to transactional analysis we have five conditioned 'drivers'. Do you recognise any of these in you? Be strong; be perfect; try hard; hurry up; please others. Essentially, we are living our life to please others, rather than living our own life.

In his book *Magical Mind, Magical Body*, endocrinologist, teacher and best-selling author Deepak Chopra MD, discusses the 'hypnosis of social conditioning', and the need to wake up from it – otherwise you will remain stuck in this half-awake state, being kicked about like a football of childhood conditioning, never realising your full potential and God-given birthright.

Basically, we experience conflicts between two parts of our make up – conscious and unconscious. These conflicts are reflected throughout our body's musculature, internal organs and nervous system, causing interference to the free flow of energy in the body. Because, in our modern society, intellect is given a higher status than our emotions, we tend to partition our emotional experience from our thinking. By suppressing our emotions – sitting firmly on any rising waves, whilst 'acting' in life in a 'reasonable, rational' way, we are suppressing our spirit, our joy – who we really are. Trapping emotional energy like this causes it to build up in the body and then it expresses itself through muscular tension, aches, pains, dreams, anxieties, neuroses, depression or physical illnesses and allergies.

From this blinkered state we make judgements and hold prejudices that fit in with our conditioned viewpoint ('drivers'), constantly evaluating things as right or wrong, good or bad. Classifying, labelling, analysing; creating turbulence in the mind. This 'head fever' constricts the flow of energy between oneself and one's connection to nature, of which horses are a part. On the other hand, non-judgement creates silence in your mind.

Defencelessness

Defencelessness means relinquishing the need to convince or persuade others of your point of view. People spend 99 per cent of their time defending their point, but if they relinquished their attachment to it they would gain access to enormous amounts of energy that had previously been wasted. When you become defensive – blame others – your life meets resistance. If you force the situation the resistance will only increase. Be like a reed that bends with the storm and survives, rather than a tall oak that cracks and collapses.

When you catch yourself judging, who is it doing the catching? This is your still point, your sixth sense, your true essence beyond ego. Fearless, free, immune to criticism; beneath no-one, superior to no-one and full of magic, mystery and enchantment. It is the level that the horse whisperer and the great riding masters work from. It is the subtle level of 'you' that is often drowned out by the noisy internal dialogue of your mind.

> Nature's intelligence functions with effortless ease. Grass doesn't try to grow, it just grows like flowers they just bloom. So when things don't go your way for the moment let go of the way you think they should be and realise that there may be a bigger picture . . . The known is our past. The known is nothing other than the prison of past conditioning . . . stagnation, entropy, disorder, and decay. Uncertainty on the other hand, is the fertile ground of freedom. Stepping into the unknown in every moment of our existence, ever fresh, ever new, always opens us to the creation of new manifestations . . . without uncertainty life is just the stale repetition of outworn memories. You become the victim of the past and your tormentor today is your self left over from yesterday.
>
> *Deepak Chopra*

You move from one bondage to another due to fear of freedom.

P. R. Shankar

Food for Thought

When you are having riding lessons, how do you feel towards your teacher? Do you want to please them? Do you want to do your best for them? How about when you are riding and training your horse, what do you expect from him?

Usually, people's response to the last question is something like: 'Well, I certainly don't want to please my horse. He has to please me.'

Why do we want to please our teacher, but not our horse? Throughout the ages, the most renowned equestrians – Xenophon, Podhajsky, de la Guérinière – have revered their horses as their greatest teachers. By stepping onto the same pathways that the great masters trod you will enter the magical journey that dressage has to offer, beautifully expressed in the following excerpt from Isenbart and Buhrer's *The Kingdom of the Horse*:

> Dressage is the return of freedom. Dressage is common purpose. Man on horseback: a twofold bond, two hearts and one mind. The equine being, master of his faculties, agile, proud, free – this creature, joined to the human being, both grown into one entity, must again become free, proud, agile, the master of its faculties! Long patient training, in the process of which it becomes impossible to identify the one or the other as teacher or pupil, culminates in the work of art which is man on horseback. Development of the strength that enables the horse to bear weight, mutual appreciation leading to obedience, delicate interchange of signals rendering communication invisible – these are the ways and means.

THE COST OF CONFORMITY

. . . most of our energy goes into upholding our importance. . . If we were capable of losing some of that importance, two extra-ordinary things would happen to us. One, we would free our energy from trying to maintain the illusory idea of our grandeur; and two, we would provide ourselves with enough energy to . . . catch a glimpse of the actual grandeur of the universe.

Don Juan to Carlos Castaneda – The Art of Dreaming

If hard, closed-minded trainers of horses would get their heads out of the sand and become more experienced in these more subtle areas of life, advanced riding would not be only the realm of the lucky few, and the lucky few would have a much happier lot!

If riders are not made consciously aware of the teaching/learning process, they remain asleep; totally dependent on the teacher, and at the teacher's mercy. Instructors would, I hope, be the first to admit that they are not God. Question them if they are not being absolutely clear. If you see them abusing your horse, change them immediately. Are you and your horse not worth more?

Ignorant, abusive training methods, promoting acrobatics rather than art, kill the very spirit of dressage and horsemanship.

These days I choose to spend a great proportion of my time working remedially with horses; those who have been at the mercy of man, and whom man has failed. Horses shipped in from abroad, homesick, disorientated, asked to perform physical impossibilities and then punished for failing by tyrants who call themselves trainers but who are totally lacking biomechanical knowledge. Slapped straight into competition they are expected to perform because of the price on their head, and quickly, while their glorious paces are still present. Vulnerable, idolising owners are swept along by the tide.

Let us go more deeply into the more subtle damage that incorrect training can cause in your horse.

Imprisoned in the Body

The 'startle response' is the body's way of responding to sudden shock. The human response involves tightening and shortening of the neck, pulling the head back and down, and lifting of the shoulders (see Figure 9; Photo 11). In addition there is a strong fear reflex that makes the body pull down into a foetal position for protection.

A horse in startle response goes above the bit, hollows, and trails his quarters. He protects himself the only way he knows how; by tightening his muscles to form an armour. Body-armouring is often mistaken for laziness. A horse displaying body-armouring is in startle response. This natural fear response has its origin in the days when our horses' ancestors were the prey of big cats and wolves. Modern horses are no longer under threat from such predators. Ironically, their new enemies are the very riders who love and care for them unaware that they are 'attacking' them with their tense riding style.

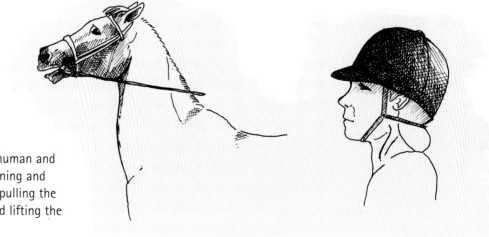

Figure 9
The startle response in human and horse. Both show tightening and shortening of the neck, pulling the head back and down and lifting the shoulders.

The human startle response is often clearly visible in novice riders. In advanced riders, it is less obvious but still present in a subtler form – and the horse feels it. If the startle response is not eliminated every time you ride, you and your horse will habitually carry yourselves rigidly, even when fear is not apparent. You know what it feels like: the horse's mouth is jammed up against the bit and he has no free forward movement; your shoulders are lifted, your back stiff and you are out of kilter with the horse.

Photo 11
The human startle response.

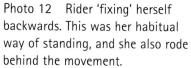

Photo 12 Rider 'fixing' herself backwards. This was her habitual way of standing, and she also rode behind the movement.

Photo 13
Rider's posture after releasing her 'fix'.

Do Short Cuts Work?

Draw reins are used to counteract the startle response by forcing the horse into the opposite shape – a rounded outline (see Figure 10). The horse, being a fight or flight creature, responds either by pushing against the pull of the draw reins, developing the wrong muscles, or by escaping behind the bit through overbending. By using draw reins you are, in fact, training the horse to evade. Ironically, in forcing the horse into a 'desirable' outline, you are creating even more problems for yourself. Look at any symptomatic approach, for example taking a sleeping pill for insomnia. Does it cure your insomnia? Or taking a tranquilliser – does this remove the source of anxiety? These approaches may cover up the symptoms, but they don't get to the root of the problem. And draw reins, like drugs, can have unpleasant and dangerous side-effects.

Working with osteopath Timothy Marris, I made a study of the effects of draw reins on horses. I am now convinced that out of expert hands their use is indefensible, and even then they should be used only once or twice to get the attention of a 'bolshy' horse while asking him to drop his nose and listen. They should never be used to shorten and draw in the neck.

Draw reins, far from being aids to training, are restrictive and potentially harmful instruments that create pain and tension. They may cause or exacerbate a variety of undesirable conditions, ranging from headaches to breathing difficulties and lameness. Marris and I arrived at these conclusions after examining a horse before, during and after the use of draw reins. According to Marris, the pull of the draw rein creates excessive flexion to the vertebra of the poll and upper neck. The resulting pressure on the brain could give the horse a headache and worsen any existing weakness of the spine. Furthermore, the strain is passed back along the neck and spine to the pelvis, causing restriction of breathing, tightening of the lower ribs and tension in the back muscles. Marris says the disturbance of the nerve supply to the front legs could easily cause lameness in the front limbs.

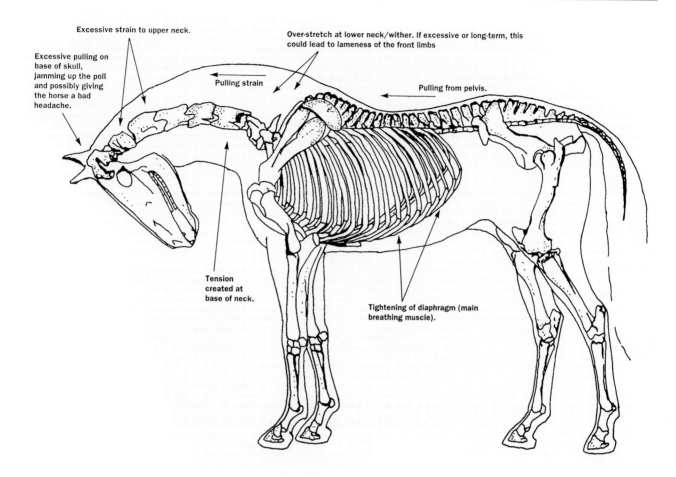

Excessive strain to upper neck.

Over-stretch at lower neck/wither. If excessive or long-term, this could lead to lameness of the front limbs

Excessive pulling on base of skull, jamming up the poll and possibly giving the horse a bad headache.

Pulling strain

Pulling from pelvis.

Tension created at base of neck.

Tightening of diaphragm (main breathing muscle).

Figure 10
The anatomical consequences of using draw reins.

The most saddening and disappointing effect of such gadgets (including tight side reins), is that they make it *more difficult* for the horse's back to raise into flexion, so the hind legs struggle to step under. And what effect does this constant pain and restraint have on the horse's spirit and well-being?

De la Guérinière said: 'Suppleness and lack of constraint are the pre-requisites for voluntarily offered obedience, not for agonised subjection of the horse being ridden'! By trapping horses in at the front you distort the way they use their quarters. To make a mechanical comparison, if a horse cannot work freely behind, his engine is choked up, his timing out; he is literally 'back-firing.' Here is a typical scenario arising from abuse of this sort, reported by Wendy, who came on my workshop at Willington Hall in Cheshire.

My horse was purchased from an Advanced level dressage rider, who had imported him from Germany as a three-year-old. He was sold on to me after competing at Elementary level. His owner felt that his paces were not extravagant enough to go beyond Medium.

He came to me a very unhappy horse, being the subject of 'lobotomy' jokes, and appearing totally unaware of his surroundings. His eyes were permanently dull, with a glazed expression. He tensed himself so much when ridden that his breathing sounded like short, shallow gasps. He was so crooked behind that he was accused of being crippled, and was referred to numerous vets and chiropractors. His movement had been blocked so much that his hind feet stepped out to the side instead of forwards. His trot was so strange that it took me two months to be able to balance on him for more than one circuit of the arena. His canter was more like a 'rock-hop' action, rather than forwards.

Within a few weeks, he broke down totally, bucking and rearing so violently when asked to go forwards, even in walk, that it became impossible for me to ride him. This was the result of being 'strangled' both mentally and physically. The mental aspect proved the more difficult to overcome as he had been imprisoned in a silent, painful world; trapped, suffering silently, as he continued to do whatever was asked of him, despite the consequences to himself.

I was worried about going on Joni's workshop as I didn't want either myself or my horse to feel any more pressure. Joni was marvellous; she encouraged an atmosphere of support and understanding and made both horse and rider feel at home. The whole ambience throughout the course felt almost spiritual and provoked a deeper awareness. Joni concentrated on the problems which were blocking horse and rider combinations from progressing. In our case, straightening my horse. The techniques Joni introduced were new to everyone on the workshop. However, they were simple to apply, even for a novice, and such common sense! We worked with basic principles such as interpressure, concentrating on balancing the horse on all four legs equally.

After two days it was very rewarding to see and feel my horse moving straight, forward and balanced – techniques that actually worked!!

The rider relaxation exercises are useful tools that I now use practically every day, and not solely in connection with riding. Employing the methods I learnt to relax and balance my horse's body meant that he had a new sense of freedom and began to enjoy being ridden, helping him to trust the directions I was giving him. I went home feeling a much stronger person, and bonded with my horse.

He is now a happy horse. I know because I can see it in his cheerful face and attitude to life. Day by day his paces become more extravagant, forward and straight.

SWITCH ON YOUR BRAIN

The rider must offer his mind to guide the body of the horse, while both of their spirits are animated by the joy of this partnership. . . . So it transpires that beauty is born of the well-honed mind of a human guiding the strong limbs of his mount into a powerful stride. . .

Charles de Kunffy

In the scheme of nature we are a privileged species. We have the ability to become aware of ourselves and therefore we are infinite choice-makers. In every moment of our existence, we make some choices consciously and others unconsciously, as discussed in the previous chapter. Whether you like it or not, everything that is happening to you at this moment is a result of the choices you've made in the past. Most of us – even though we are infinite choice-makers – have become bundles of unconscious, conditioned reflexes that are constantly being triggered by people and circumstances.

I'll bet that, like me, when you are watching show jumping you find yourself leaping and jumping about on your chair. This is a simple example of losing our sense of self, our 'centredness', and relinquishing our energy to an object of reference – in this case the horse and rider who are jumping. This is all right and good fun while we are watching show jumping but if this sort of thing is happening unconsciously in our everyday life, we will be wasting energy and losing vitality. Keeping your identity centred within yourself helps you to retain your energy and preserve your power.

Figure 11   Our unconscious, conditioned reflexes are constantly being triggered by people and circumstances.

Stopping

When I began my Alexander teacher training course it soon became horribly clear how much I pulled myself around. No wonder I used to get so exhausted while teaching riding. I found myself gripping my stomach, 'scrunching' my upper body down towards my pelvis and yanking my head and neck back while instructing. My back, neck and legs were often clamped. Living your life in this way causes unnecessary strain in the nervous system resulting in stress, ill-health and exhaustion. Now when I catch myself in this situation I observe it and then choose to let go. Immediately I stop straining I become taller, more open and 'present in the world'. I become a conscious choice-maker and it is very empowering. So, when you catch yourself in this situation, use the following four-step programme:

1. Pause.
2. Notice where you feel tight – mentally, physically or emotionally.
3. Choose to let go of the tightness – it's as simple as unclenching a clenched fist
4. Bring your attention out into the world again.

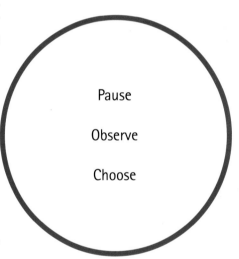

Learning Through Games

I use a game in my workshops to illustrate to people how they react automatically and without thinking to outer stimuli because of fear of failing in their peers' eyes. Try this game with your friends and see if you can catch yourself in the act. To explain it I'll use names for different players.

Sit in a circle on chairs. One person starts: Mary looks at Susan, says Susan's name and gets up and moves to Susan's chair to sit in it. Before vacating her chair, Susan looks at Dorothy, says Dorothy's name and moves to sit in Dorothy's chair. Before she leaves her chair, Dorothy looks at Lisa, calls Lisa's name and moves to sit in Lisa's chair – and so on, in a chain. The aim is to keep on moving.

Photo 14   The chair game.

Our failures are stepping stones bringing us ever closer to our goal.

Students report a number of very common experiences. First, they react without thinking and panic about holding up the game; they worry about keeping people waiting or getting it wrong and looking stupid. Unfortunately, this hurry-up syndrome is what disconnects us from our centre and results in bad use of the body. Second, they feel nervous in the pit of their stomach. Third, they hold their breath. Fourth, they always pick the same person or the one in front of them. Fifth, they get out of their chair in panic and find themselves in the middle of the room with nowhere to go because they forgot to call someone's name out first. Sixth, they feel exhausted.

As the game progresses, I reassure them that it's OK to get it wrong, and remind them that our failures are stepping-stones, bringing us ever closer to our goals. In reality there is no such thing as failure. What we call failure is just a mechanism through which we can learn to do things right. Next, I teach them to centre themselves and heighten their awareness of their mind, body and breathing. Then, the game begins to flow more: they pause and think before they move. This pause gives the students time to allow the conditioned response to dissolve before they act. They can choose consciously without panic where to move and, when they do move, they give themselves breath and use their bodies well.

Just as humans can panic and suffer stress when performance is expected, so can horses. The game I have described shows that we can believe we are thinking clearly when in fact we are victims of unconscious, knee-jerk panic responses. The game gives the student an insight into how a horse may be confused or upset by his rider's unclear signals, and so set up a resistance against the rider.

A Case Study

Audrey wanted to progress much faster in her dressage than she was ready for. Speaking to her I discovered that her life had recently become very stressful. The pressure of it had pulled her out of her sense of self. She was being tossed around like a piece of flotsam in a storm – and this had disturbed her peace of mind. Because she was getting older she was desperate to be a successful rider before it was too late.

Things were made worse when she met up with her old teacher, Sue who, like Audrey, was caught up in a whirlwind of activity: very busy, no time for herself, always rush, rush, rush. Because Sue runs her life at such a hectic pace, she made Audrey feel guilty, selfish and unrealistic about looking after herself – when that's really what Sue secretly wanted and needed more than anything. What we dislike in others is what we secretly and unconsciously deny in ourselves.

Ironically, rushing in riding is counter-productive because the other side of the partnership – the horse – will not co-operate. If he is rushed, he will react with nervousness and resistance, which makes training harder for both horse and rider.

After her encounter with Sue, I had to build Audrey's confidence up again and started by renewing her awareness of her mind/body connection. I began with an Alexander lesson on the wooden horse. I asked her to deliberately think about something in the future and to notice how her body responded.

'It's all tightened up,' said Audrey, 'and I've lifted myself up off the saddle.'

'OK,' I said. 'Now come into the present – where you actually are – into this room with me.'

'That's better – now I've relaxed, I feel lighter and freer', she said. She also noticed that she was much happier when she was present with me rather than time-travelling in her mind – there was no fear. Thinking into the future activated her body's fear reflexes.

'Now,' I said, 'go back in time to a lesson with Sue.'

She closed her eyes, and as she visualised the lesson, she

noticed that her mind was in the future, focused on a mental image of what she wanted rather than what she had. She was shocked when she realised how totally unaware she was of the horse; how he felt, how he was moving. She felt tense, and had retreated from the world around her: she was totally oblivious to her surroundings.

I asked her to describe the place she was in when she narrowed herself down like this. The first thing that sprang to her mind was 'lonely.' Her body reflected the tension of her mind: her neck was tight, her spine shortened, her pelvic floor tightened. Her legs were pulled up, causing her seat to be tense. There was no movement in her hips, and her seat bones tensed down into the saddle. If this had been a real horse he would have hollowed away; her hands were fixed and would block the forward motion of the horse. Emotionally, she was angry and frustrated.

'Now,' I said, 'come into the present moment – here with me in the room.'

'Phew,' said Audrey. 'What a relief to let go of all that. Why do we do it?'

'Because of a lifetime of conditioning. The more you become aware of your conditioning the more you can liberate yourself from its pitfalls. Now let's take this exercise onto your real horse and see what happens.'

As Audrey rode around the arena, I kept opening her up out into the world as she was tending to look inward. To help her to keep 'present' I suggested she use an image that one of my students, Alison Skeats, came up with. Imagine you have blinds on the back of your eyeballs, and you have shut them down so that you can only look outwards. It worked a treat: the mare opened up her stride as she opened up herself. However, a few minutes later the horse started playing up and I noticed anger bubbling up in Audrey. She was transferring deeply suppressed anger onto her mare, so I asked her what was happening.

'My horse won't listen to me. It's not fair! Every day I feed her and look after her, and she can't even give me her attention. She'd rather look at the horse in the next field.'

'And where are you now?' I asked. Audrey noticed immediately that she was in the past, thinking about what the horse owed her – her part of the deal. Unfortunately, the horse was unaware of this contract.

'OK. Come back into the present with me and the horse in the arena. Do you think you are projecting human values and concepts onto your horse? Do you think she knows about social niceties? Is she human – or an animal?'

Audrey realised that her reactions had been inappropriate and that if she really wanted a happy, successful life and to achieve her goals she had to look to herself and stop blaming others. Losing your temper and firing off onto the nearest person or horse – laying blame – only worsens the situation. It may make you feel better temporarily but it doesn't help you to grow. Instead of trying to change others – which is very difficult – it is more useful to change the way you look at things. This is because people, things, and circumstances change and often they are only mirroring to you your own hurt, doubt and disappointment buried deep in your nervous system (see Chapter 5 – Transactional Analysis).

Audrey felt sorry and stroked the horse. 'Who are you really angry with?' I asked. Audrey replied sarcastically, 'Have you got all day?'

I gave her a simple yogic breathing technique to release anger and stress. At first, she found this difficult to do and burst out laughing – the trapped emotions were beginning to release. Her face softened and she looked at least ten years younger – and so did the horse! I told her that usually horses will spook if the rider pressurises them too much: they are literally running away from the pressure.

She carried on riding and after a few more minutes cried out: 'What's happening? What do I look like? Am I doing it right? My body's just gone into a rhythm.' She was rising to the trot in a beautiful position, totally in the movement and in harmony with her horse – and the horse was on the bit. Audrey's next comment was revealing: 'I can't believe it. I haven't done any-thing. My body is doing it itself!' I reminded her of what Alexander had said: 'Stop doing the wrong thing and the right thing does itself.' This was no miracle. She was experiencing the fruits of being a conscious choice-maker.

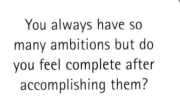

You always have so many ambitions but do you feel complete after accomplishing them?

P. R. Shankar

CHAPTER 8

DO LESS, ACCOMPLISH MORE

You can never through violence cause the horse to perfect the manner in which it expresses its skill, but only by delicate alternation between coaxing and demanding, between much praise and little punishment.

Podhajsky

Training must be carried out through liberation, not restriction. Releasing the body's natural inner energy is what creates lightness and the lift we call elevation. On the other hand, muscular tightness, a result of hard, restrictive training methods, has the effect of locking in and trapping this powerful inner energy, causing a stiff, heavy action.

I was called in to help a top dressage rider with hip pain. Before whisking me off to the house to cure her problems, she briefly introduced me to her horse. Before me stood one of the most pitiful, dejected creatures I think I have ever met. I'm going to call him Monarch for confidentiality reasons.

Monarch was totally oblivious to the fact that we had entered his stable; he just stood locked into his own world, staring vacantly at the wall. I stroked him and talked to him. Nothing. The owner had absolutely no relationship with the horse, to her this behaviour was normal. As my heart went out to him she babbled on about how happy she was with her current trainer because, although she thought he was a bit hard, they were doing well in competition. After seeing the condition this creature was in, this made me wonder who she was being judged by.

I gave her a lesson on the wooden horse and realigned her body, releasing her right problem hip. Impressed with the results, she asked me to watch her ride. On the way back to the stable she asked if I could improve her horse's performance the way I had improved hers so miraculously.

'What is the difference between a human's body and a horse's?' I asked her. 'They are both vertebrates – one on a vertical plane and the other horizontal'.

I asked her whether the horse was always so switched off, to which she replied: 'Oh yes! Like most high level horses; they have to be disciplined – I'm in with the big boys now!' She then proceeded to drag all kinds of tack out of her cupboard and tacked him up, while I stood there quietly watching. First the draw reins, then spurs, and lastly two very long, thin schooling whips.

Finally, in his full attire, he was ready. As this poor creature snapped back to the land of the living, dragging himself with great effort out of the stable, stiff as a plank, joints cracking and clicking, she whipped him violently. Monarch winced and jumped to attention with a deep grunt. His eyes were pitiful. 'He's so lazy' she said, self-righteously.

I'd seen enough. I knew it was no use telling her off because she was only doing what she believed was right (see Chapter 5 – archaic parent conditioning). This ignorance is rife in the competition world where ego and attitude abound – the only thing that matters is the ribbons. Before he had gone more than ten steps into the yard I told her to stop, bring the horse back and untack him. When she asked why, I explained that it was obvious he was unlevel and badly in need of some Alexander work to realign *his body*.

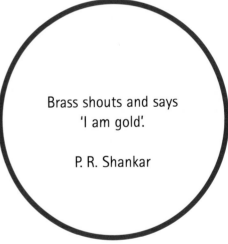

Brass shouts and says
'I am gold'.

P. R. Shankar

Working on the horse, I could feel his abdominal area solidly knotted up with stress and tension; there was no movement as he breathed in and out. I placed my other hand on his thoracic spine, which she had obviously been pulverising with grinding, uneven seat bones. Eventually he began to notice the presence of my hands on his back and belly and released his breathing mechanism and abdomen a little. As I continued to work on him I explained to her why he was 'lazy'. I knew that the horse would need a lot of time to let go, so I thought I'd better amuse her and educate her at the same time.

I explained that good and correct training of horses is sadly lacking. Riders and trainers try to emulate top-class riders like

Arthur Kottas and Reiner Klimke by attempting to duplicate the image they see in front of them – the problem, however, is that what they are seeing is the finished article, without the creative process that produced it. Unlike Arthur Kottas and Reiner Klimke, less experienced riders who are trying to mimic them end up, out of frustration, pulling the horse's head into his neck, driving him into a so-called 'contact' with legs of steel, spanking along much too fast, pushing the horse more and more onto his forehand and out of his natural stride and rhythm, thereby making self-carriage impossible. The failing student, already blue in the face, is 'spurred on' by the instructor and told that *one day*, when their legs are strong enough, they will get their horse 'on the bit'.

Monarch relaxed more and started to let go of his abdominal muscles. I began to feel some life come back into his body under my hands; his neck and back started to lengthen and widen and his sides started to move.

'Isn't true self-carriage a thing of beauty and grace, not strain and force?' I asked her. She looked distant. I think she had labelled me as an animal rights maniac. Another grunt from Monarch. I asked her to bring me a couple of books I had noticed in her library, accompanied by a cup of tea.

'What does Oliveira say about use of the leg and hands?' I asked her. She dived into Nuno Oliveira's *Reflections of Equestrian Art*.

> What is essential is not to tighten the legs during the dressage training, but to use them without effort while allowing them to hang softly near the horse's sides. The rider's leg must adhere totally to the horse without any muscular contraction, which will ensure a supple application of the legs when needed, and to which the horse responds smoothly without either rigidity or harshness, or in rejecting the action of the rider's legs.
>
> If the hands harden, they tend to keep the horse from going forward. Only the rider who is free from any contraction will have a horse equally free from contraction. A team such as this is the ideal . . . It is this total ease and relaxation which makes the rider as one with his horse, without hindering any movement . . . It is only by rational and calm methods which are never brutal that the horse may become obedient and well balanced.

Figure 12
The 'failing' student.

Oliveira then goes on to say that, in *Exterieur et Haute Ecole*, Captain Beudant writes: 'It is only by allowing horses to move on a free rein, and not in holding them in, that success may be obtained. Riders who hold in their horses are insignificant riders and will never advance. Riders who give their horses freedom are those who will taste the delicacies of equestrian art.'

My client then piped up: 'But he won't move unless I use force. This isn't a perfect world you know.'

'I know, and that is why I am working on him now, dismounted, because tense training methods result in a syndrome known as body-armouring. It's easily recognisable by the horse's short, graceless stride and dull eye and that is exactly what is wrong with Monarch.'

Body-armouring is often mistaken for laziness, for which the remedy used is more force; the vicious circle continues. I explained the startle response, and how, because trainers and riders are unaware of this syndrome, they resort to quick-fix approaches such as draw reins. But in doing so, they create more problems than they solve.

Monarch started to take up some strange breathing patterns, heaving and grunting. She viewed him with mild interest – her body-armouring was definitely well established. I continued to work on him. I think by now she had a small pang of conscience, as it was dawning on her that Monarch was actually flesh and blood and had a nervous system and emotions.

'You know, horses suffering from colic are often holding stress and tension in their guts', I informed her.

'Oh, that's why Monarch is so prone to colic' she said, softly.

I glanced over at the draw reins lying on the door. 'How often, and for how long, do you use those?' I asked.

'Oh, every day for about an hour; he won't work in an outline without them. It's either that or a double.' I explained to her my research with Tim Marris.

I paused a moment. Monarch started to pant and contract his head and neck back and up – she watched in amazement. He was beginning to correct the delicate postural reflexes that had been upset by the force and strain of draw reins and rough training. I stayed with him as he continued to extend and untwist his knotted spine for about five minutes, then he dropped his head. His breathing had now changed to very slow and deep. I warned her that he had released an enormous amount of emotional, muscular, armouring and that he should now be turned out and given time to integrate the changes for a week, after which she would find him a different horse to ride. With some armouring released it wouldn't be necessary to use the whips, spurs or draw reins. I also suggested that she take a long, cool look at the words of the great masters:

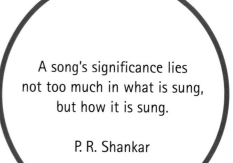

A song's significance lies not too much in what is sung, but how it is sung.

P. R. Shankar

Gentleness – is it worthwhile? Yes, always! Yes, it is worthwhile to 'put on bedroom slippers' as Baucher advises, and to try to ride all horses, without exception, using the reins and the legs with the utmost gentleness and the least effort. We must not be deceived by apparently rapid results obtained by the use of violence.

Nuno Oliveira

The earth doesn't try to spin on its own axis; it is the nature of the earth to spin with dizzying speed and to hurtle through space. It is the nature of the sun to shine, the stars to glitter and sparkle . . . Nature's intelligence functions effortlessly . . . it is intuitive, holistic, and nourishing and when you are in harmony with nature . . . established in the knowledge of your true self, you can make use of the law of least effort: 'do less and accomplish more'.

Deepak Chopra

Eight days later, my client phoned me to book a riding lesson.

CHAPTER

9

MIND-HOPPING

If you stop fighting and resisting you will experience fully the present, which is a gift. The past is history, the future is a mystery and this moment is a gift. That is why this moment is called the 'present'.

Deepak Chopra

By now you are probably beginning to realise that the root of all tension lies in the mind. This being so, correcting specific positional problems, for example raised, tense shoulders, collapsed hips, etc. unfortunately does not deal with the root cause of the tension.

You may know a lot about your body position from horse training, but do you realise that your mind has three positions – past, present and future? While you have been reading this page, for example, have you noticed whether your mind has been wandering off onto other thoughts? Has it been hopping from the past into the future and back again. Perhaps: 'I hope there are no flags at the competition tomorrow (future), he always spooks at them (past) and I'll probably fall off and miss work on Monday (future).' Where is your mind right now? Are you fully with these words right now; 100 per cent . . . 50 per cent . . . 30 per cent . . . or less? Or are you being distracted and going off on other thoughts?

When you have 100 per cent of your attention on these words you are in the present moment without any mental interference. Mind-hopping, however, causes stresses to build up in your nervous system. The emotions often attached to the past are regret, anger and disappointment, and to the future, anxiety. As the past has gone and the future is not under your control, mind-hopping is a pointless waste of energy. We worry our-selves to exhaustion, usually over nothing. If you don't believe me go into a room and deliberately worry 100 per cent for 30 minutes, then notice how drained you feel. Did it help you to win your future dressage test, or stop you from knocking down your last jump?

When you are worried, you literally shrink away from the world around you into your own little world, like Audrey did (see Chapter 7). You shrink to such an extent that you often lose sight of your surroundings, for example the person who walks straight into a lamp-post, nearly knocking them-selves out – it soon brings them back to present reality! Another example is when you know the dressage test or the jumping course by heart, but you still go the wrong way.

If your mind is not present – not 'here' – how can your feel your horse's paces? How can you ride to your full potential? Mentally trapped in the past, or the future, wound up with the pressure of modern-day living, you are literally 'up-tight' – your mental turbulence is registering itself in your body, hence the tight shoulders and crooked position. And the horse feels it; this makes him nervous and tense.

Figure 13
Emotions attached to the past and future.

Where is your mind right now? Are you still with me com-pletely? When the horse feels tension from the rider, he doesn't think, as humans might, 'Well, she's worried about her dressage test next week' or 'It must be that phone call from her boyfriend yesterday that upset her.' All that reaches him is pure tension, passing from your body to his in the form of minute physiolog-ical signals. He concludes, perhaps, that there must be a mon-ster behind the nearest bush. Result – a jittery horse. If he is a brave horse, for whom monsters hold no terror, then at the very least he feels tense seat bones digging into his sensitive back, and hollows away. Result – an uncomfortable and therefore uncooperative horse.

Because your mind is hopping around communication becomes unclear, so how can your aids be clear. You are now into the all-too-familiar downward spiral of frustration, aggression and over-domination, of which the results are misunderstanding and grief; riding becomes a battle rather than a joy.

To avoid the creation of mental and physical tension, not only in riding but also in life, we must develop the ability to observe our mind and make it work for us rather than against us. Here are three ways of doing so.

Observing It

Figure 14
Only when you are in the present moment will you know exactly what you need to do to reach your goal.

Once you have read this chapter you will catch yourself mind-hopping more and more in your daily life. When your mind is projected into the future you will feel some discomfort, some inner tension, worry, and that's your signal. Projecting your mind into the future in this way is what Alexander called 'end-gaining'. Many students have had it so drummed into them to hammer the horse forward that they have been conditioned to project their mind into the future – to establish a constant inner tension. The horse responds to this tension by establishing a permanent startle response and losing his self-carriage. Only by detaching your mind from this tension, releasing it into the present moment can you release your physical tension, and be fully aware of what is happening to you right now – and only when you are in the present moment will you know exactly what you need to do to reach your goal.

Letting go of this habitual tension is not easy for some riders, because they have been programmed into believing that tension is a good thing; that they need it to be an effective rider. In fact, what they really need is to replace this automatic tension response with intelligent, focused energy. Alexander called this using the 'means whereby' that is, the means whereby you get to your goal.

Ironically, people who manage to let go of the hurry-up syndrome and learn to work patiently with the means whereby are frequently surprised by how easily and rapidly the results come. They've found that being fully aware of what is happening in their own and their horse's mind and body, right now, is the best starting point to get to the goal. It's like when you're trying to find your way to a certain town. The surest way to get there quickly is to look at a map to establish where you are right now.

Discriminating Between Desire and Intention

There is a difference between a desire (end-gaining) and an intention (means whereby.) All good work happens through intention. You intend – 'I want to go somewhere' – you go. All life moves with intention. If I don't have an intention to raise my hand it will not raise.

Desire is that intention turning into a feverish thought in you. A desire is a thought with feverishness coming in you again and again that shakes the whole nervous system. Desire brings a dis-ease in the mind, an obsession in the mind. It clouds the clarity of the mind. It brings feverishness and burns. It leaves you with scars and wounds. Every frustration, every desire has caused stress in the nervous system, and you are not even aware of it. The first time you become aware of it – 'Oh there are a lot of things here I have done to myself' – then you clear it up.

Ravi Shankar *Bang on the Door*

Xenophon pointed out that reliance on 'quick-fix' training methods short-circuits the learning process and aborts the birth of a real understanding between horse and rider. He said that over two thousand years ago – yet still we are using force and constraint in training horses. How far have we really progressed in our philosophy of horsemanship?

What happens in horse terms if you use end-gaining rather than the means whereby? You are ahead of the horse in time and space, and not attentive to how you can help him in the present moment. End-gaining is inappropriate in training. The end-gaining rider fails in at least three ways:

1. By attempting to force the horse to do things for which his training has not prepared him.

2. By assuming that the horse has human feelings, motives and intelligence.

3. By judging the horse according to his or her own emotional conditioning – and often shifting the responsibility for what is happening onto the horse.

Release Stress – Experience the Present

What are the advantages of living in the present moment? A silent, uncluttered mind; a listening point; heightened sensory appreciation; fulfilment, joy and confidence; reduced stress and depression; unlimited potential, because in this word-less state you can access the wisdom of the body (cellular memory).

Here is an exercise to make the present moment become your living reality. Use this breathing technique daily for about twenty minutes at home. It's an ancient breathing technique. We'll call it the 'Darth Vader breath'. *Star Wars* fans will explain why. People naturally breathe like this when they're asleep. The breath becomes longer and more efficient, and audible to the horse. This calms him and, at the same time, releases stress from both your nervous system and his. My students find it a brilliant way of integrating themselves in stressful situations, for example at their workplace, or during a horse trial. It's also a brilliant pick-me-up if you're tired. Find yourself a warm room where you will not be disturbed and make yourself comfortable. Keep your back as straight as is comfortable.

Close your eyes and take your attention to your breathing. Open your mouth and relax your jaw down gently as if you are yawning slightly. Make an audible, whispered, breathy 'ahhhh' sound as you exhale, and then on inhalation until you are breathing easily like Darth Vader ... Then, half-way through the exhalation, close your lips together and breathe, so you are now breathing in and out through your nose. If you have problems making the sound, make a snoring sound from your throat first, and then tone it down.

Figure 15
The advantages of living in the present moment.

If you find your breathing jerky, or you can't make the sound as you inhale, you need to work at it more – this is a sign that you have been holding tension there.

To follow each of the instructions below allow yourself at least two minutes.

- Now as you are breathing – effortlessly – notice the thoughts in your head. Think of them as visitors to your house: and observe them passing by (two minutes).

- Notice the sounds around you (two minutes).

- Now take your attention to your body. Allow your attention to drift effortlessly to any physical sensations. Any anxiety in the mind will have its physical counterpart. It could be tightness or tingling in the stomach or chest. Allow your attention to rest on the physical sensations without judging them. Allow any feelings you have to express themselves. Welcome them. What you resist persists. (Allow at least five minutes).

Slowly start to breathe normally again, keeping your eyes closed.

Do you notice any quietness inside (one minute)?

Notice the thoughts in your head (one minute).

Become aware of your surroundings (one minute).

Open your eyes very slowly (and give yourself at least two minutes before you open your eyes).

You can use the following process with your eyes open whilst riding to help your mind be present and open:

Look around at your surroundings.

Use all your senses.

Notice all the colours and textures around you. Look at them as though for the first time.

Listen to the sounds.

Smell the different aromas.

Feel the warmth and support of your horse underneath you. Allow that support to melt up into you, right to the top of your head.

To bring you even more present, if it's safe to do so, clap your hands loudly; you can even pat your horse – I'm sure he will appreciate it.

According to *The Principles of Riding*, the official instruction handbook of the German National Equestrian Federation:

> Only the relaxed rider can sit in a secure balance, and only when this is achieved can the trainer start to refine the rider's position. The cause of most seat faults is the rider's failure to relax. Therefore the first thing that a rider has to learn is a completely relaxed seat. Only when he has achieved this can he be taught position.

Here again are the three tools to put you in control of your life.

1. Use the four-step programme.
2. Discriminating between intention and desire.
3. Darth Vader breathing, to refine the awareness of observing your mind and, at the same time, to release stress from the nervous system. (Breathing in this way increased prana in the body. Prana – life-force energy – releases toxins from every cell in the body, so you may experience some tingling in the body whilst breathing in this way.)

Now, armed with this new knowledge, you can open the door to real progress in the relationship between you and your horse and fulfil the vision of the great masters of horsemanship. By fine-tuning our sensitivity and understanding of ourselves we can then find out where we are going wrong.

CHAPTER 10

DROP THE 'IDEAL' AND GET 'REAL'

If we promote riding with an incorrect seat, and incorrect aids, we will only have an accumulation of mistakes. The longer such people ride horses, the more damage they can inflict. Yet correct riding should produce the opposite, for classical horsemanship is therapeutic riding. It is aimed at the restorative functions of the horse's natural balance. It is therapeutically concerned with the suppleness of the spine and musculature, and the even-loading efficiencies of the hind legs.

Charles de Kunffy, The Ethics and Passions of Dressage

Books today tend to focus on the correct seat and how it 'should be', but very few on how it actually is and how to put it right. This is why Alexander's theory of letting go of your rigid attachment to your goal – how you think things 'should' be – and instead focusing on the means whereby – how they actually are – is vital.

Choose a teacher with the same philosophy. As we know, our bodies don't always behave in the way we want them to, or to command. In my case the value of Alexander's wise words was made painfully obvious. Sick of being told that I was still perching on my horse, even though I was a qualified riding instructress, I decided, at great expense, to resort to drastic measures and put myself under the guidance of a supposedly expert international trainer. Duncan, my boyfriend at the time, came with me. He had ridden as a child and done well in Pony Club.

Figure 16   The first lesson was a disaster.

The first lesson was a disaster for me. The instructress watched me with a cool quietness for a few minutes.

'OK, that will do', she shouted. 'Your rising trot is all wrong.' She demonstrated the correct way. 'This is how it should be', she said patronisingly. I tried to copy her to the best of my ability but my body just wouldn't oblige. Once again she continued to demonstrate the 'should be' rising trot, this time straddling a jump pole resting on two jump wings. Up and down she went: 'Do it like this'. I tried desperately to copy her again and again, much to the amusement of the other people in the indoor school.

'No, no, no', she said. 'Watch me and do it like this.' I tried again with all my might but I just couldn't get it; my body refused. My upper body kept tipping forwards like a horse on the forehand – I couldn't load my hindquarters at all, never mind evenly. After about half an hour she threw her hands up in the air and gave up, the failure being mine rather than her 'flaky' instruction. Duncan, wouldn't you know, had a great lesson and could do no wrong.

By now I was beginning to lose confidence in myself – perhaps I *was* a moron, with something drastically wrong with me. I dragged myself back to my room, depressed and despondent. Duncan tried to cheer me up without success.

Sunday morning arrived. The instructress didn't work on rising trot, opting for sitting. I had to take my feet out of the stirrups and raise my knees skyward what felt miles above the saddle whilst trotting around the very large indoor school. Hair-raising to say the least, especially on the long side when the horse spooked. In hindsight I realise she was teaching me the bad habit of driving with the seat (see Chapter 19 – Sitting Trot). Finally I was allowed to replace my feet in the stirrups, but not before having my legs wrenched back, much to the distress of each muscle fibre. The horse started trotting, when suddenly a blood-curdling scream attacked me from the far end of the school: 'Stop wobbling!' With determination, I made my body rigid. The scream came again; this time I screamed back at her: 'How?'

When people don't have much inside, they make a big show outside.

P. R. Shankar

'Are you stupid? Just stop', she sneered. Resigned to the fact that I wasn't going to get any help from her I managed to stop wobbling by making myself as stiff as a plank. Absorption of the movement was obviously not a priority in this school. In revenge the horse stiffened and hollowed his back, so wobbling regressed into banging. I'm sure he was as bruised as I was.

'Good', she said, 'At last you've got it! so we'll finish on a good note. You need to go back to basics', she said haughtily.

'Funny, I thought that's what I was here for', I replied. I watched her march out of the school without a care in the world as my heart sank and I choked back the tears. My big hope had just walked out of the door. In the privacy of my room, feeling violated by the sheer hardness and insensitivity of the women, I let rip, unburdening myself of all the anger, hurt, humiliation and injustice she had inflicted on me. In my heart of hearts I knew I wasn't stupid, but at the mercy of ignorant training, that merely glossed over problems rather than solving them and, what's worse, didn't care if they didn't solve them. Dressage is supposed to open spirit, not destroy it. It was time to take a different tack. It was from this moment I knew I was going to create a better way for horse and rider to enjoy their art.

The reason I was struggling so much in my lesson became apparent during my first week's training dismounted at the Alexander school: my ankles were incredibly stiff. The teacher started to work with me in 'monkey' (see Photo 15 – Alexander called this 'the position of mechanical advantage'). It suddenly became clear to me, going in and out of a chair (which is similar to rising trot), why I was perching forwards. I couldn't sit down into my body, much the same as a horse can't sit on his hocks until he is trained. Some people, like some horses, can do it more easily than others. If you can't squat without lifting your heels off the ground you need, like me, to develop more flexibility in your hips, hamstrings, knees and ankles. Watch children under the age of two – almost without exception they squat without lifting their heels off the ground. We spoil the good use of our bodies through trying too hard and too

Photo 15
Alexander working with a
young pupil in the position
of mechanical advantage.

fast, rushing around 'in front' of ourselves so to speak, like horses on the forehand who have not yet learned to carry themselves. Like horses we have to stop running, and allow our hindquarters to sit, engage, and carry us, rather than pushing ourselves stiffly along with our legs. My hamstrings and back muscles had shortened because of the bad way I used myself in life. The dismounted Alexander technique lessons taught me to centre myself and work on the means whereby you get to the 'ideal'; knowledge that the riding instructress mentioned had seriously lacked. Working in 'monkey' developed length in my back, legs and ankles so that I could release and engage my 'quarters'. I couldn't wait to ride. Just as I had suspected, riding in this way completely eliminated all my problems. I now had the ability to sit down and around the horse rather than perching on top – even the famous instructress would have been proud of my rising trot!

So, as my bitter experience shows only too painfully, drop the 'ideal' and get 'real'.

PART TWO

Journeying to the Unknown

Knowledge is like a river; the deeper it is the less noise it makes.
Strength does not worry about weight,
Enthusiasm does not worry about distance,
Wisdom does not worry about borders,
Social nature does not worry about strangeness.

Ratnananda

CHAPTER 11

To some readers, this chapter may seem a bit 'way out', but that is what it is meant to be – a way out! Read on only if you are ready.

What is the difference between a question(?) and wonder(!) ? With wonder, the ! is not bent out of shape. Questions seek answers; wonderment doesn't seek an answer. A question is related to sorrow and doubt, whereas wonder is related to joy. Do you ever ask: 'Why am I happy?' No, we usually ask why only when we are miserable: 'Why should this misery come to me?' We never question why there is so much beauty in the world, in Creation. If somebody is furious with us, we never question this reality, but if someone says they love us, we doubt it: 'Do you really love me?' When we encounter dishonesty or injustice, we ask: 'Why is it always me who suffers injustice?' This question why comes from that area of our mind that seeks to know. Factual knowledge is labelling things.

Knowledge and Wonder

To know, or not to know: that is the question! Clinging on to what you already know is very seductive and safe, so you do it. But are you advancing, nestled in your comfort zone?

Figure 17   The purpose of real knowledge is to put you in touch with yourself in the moment.

Are you broadening your vision in life? Would you keep returning to the same holiday place, year after year after year, rather than seeking new, exciting places to visit. Would this not prove a little boring? That which we already know, we speak from our intellect, which means we are drawing on the past. However, the purpose of real knowledge is to put you in touch with yourself in the moment, ever fresh, ever new – then you will come to realise how your ignorance, your conditioning, blocks your progress.

The more you know, the more you realise how much remains unknown; go to a library and look around if you doubt this. When you 'think' you know, you don't know; it is an ignorant 'understanding', not the understanding of your own ignorance. Our conditioned minds are just as unreliable as our bodies – see Chapter 4 Does Right Feel Right?' and Chapter 5 The Hypnosis of Social Conditioning.

The greatest scientists are humbled by the wonder of the unknown. They experiment to find out how things work, because they don't know. The greater the scientists, the more amazed they are by the wonder of Creation. If you ask them, when they have made some great discovery, where they learnt it from, they will tell you: 'I don't know – it just happened.'

Wonderment keeps us open; keeps our learning alive and fresh. It is the most creative thing. In wonder we drop our preconceived ideas of how we think things 'should' be. Instead, we feel, experience and recognise, living moment to moment to moment.

Blessed are those who are confused.
Confusion means your previous knowledge has broken down. Your
belief has broken down. That is a step in knowledge. Whatever I say,
whether you agree or disagree, it doesn't matter. But are you aware of
what is happening in your own mind? That is sufficient . . . Awareness
of what is happening within you, that is self-study.

P.R. Shankar

Like the great scientist, don't be ashamed to say 'I don't
know', because it leaves you open for new knowledge to flow
through you. It is only the conditioned part of you, the ego, that
makes you feel you must behave in a certain way and save face
at any cost. This makes you unnatural.

Being Natural

Ironically, we overlook the fact that it is we, who have choked our
freedom by custom and conventions under the subtle pressure of
civilization and press down our innate nature. The result is that it is
becoming very unnatural for us to be natural. As a child, we show
what we feel, but as we grow, we show off what we don't feel . . . To
show is to express, but to show off is to hide; a strong man shows, a
weak man shows off.

Ratnananda

Naturalness is the feeling of belonging; of being at home; of
feeling close to everyone. It is the ego that creates the distance.
When people have to show off or behave in a certain manner
there is no cordiality or connection with their fellows. The ego
makes you a football of others' opinions: 'Oh, what will they
think of me if I fail my exams?' 'Oh, what will they think if they
come to my house and find it in such a mess?' Shame; guilt; fear;
pretending to be something we are not, all cause separation.

What we see outside ourselves is a projection of what we see
within our own mind. We always project onto the world the
thoughts, feeling and attitudes which preoccupy us. We can see
the world differently by changing our mind about what we *want*
to see. In order to experience wonderment, we have to know our

own mind. Where are we taught to learn how to manage our minds and emotions? It wasn't part of my school curriculum. There, I was taught only how to conform to society, and to exist without being too much of a nuisance. I got a pat on the back for learning a whole bunch of facts, by rote, and running all the five drivers: try hard; hurry up; please me; be strong; be perfect (see Chapter 5), like some kind of robot. Catching ourselves behaving in this mode puts us on the journey to the unknown which is freedom and naturalness.

Opinions and Judgements

Holding on to our opinions is a complete waste of time, because our opinions change constantly. If you observe your mind, you will see it is like a roller-coaster. Life is much more charming when you let go of your opinions, having seen how they keep you stuck in your old knowledge, in the past. Your opinions block new light from flowing in by narrowing down your vision. Have you ever noticed that if you don't defend your point of view people have nothing to attack? You lose nothing and preserve your energy. Let people think what they wish; if they are rigidly attached to their point of view, reasoning with them is a waste of time anyway.

Accept people as they are. You can't change others, but you can change yourself. Look at the opinion chart (Figure 18) and construct one of your own. It's fun and enlightening at the same time.

Construct a circle split in half by a line down the middle. Starting in the bottom left half, notch up one number at a time:

1. I really like Allison; she is so helpful.
2. Allison is so supportive of me.
3. She wears such trendy clothes.
4. She is so slim.
5. She is so enthusiastic, joining in on everything.
6. She never leaves anybody out; Allison is such a wonderful person.

Continue adding your own ideas, up to a score of ten. Then start at the top right hand of the circle:

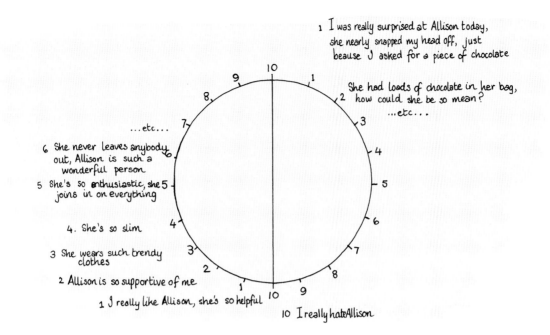

1. I was really surprised at Allison today, she nearly snapped my head off, just beause I asked for a piece of chocolate

2. She had loads of chocolate in her bag, how could she be so mean?
   ...etc...

6. She never leaves anybody out, Allison is such a wonderful person

5. She's so enthusiastic, she joins in on everything

4. She's so slim

3. She wears such trendy clothes

2. Allison is so supportive of me

1. I really like Allison, she's so helpful

10. I really hate Allison

Figure 18   Opinion chart.

1. I was really surprised at Allison yesterday; she nearly snapped my head off just because I asked for a piece of chocolate.
2. She had loads of chocolate in her bag, how could she be so mean?

Continue adding ideas until you have notched up ten negatives and reached the lowest side of the circle:

10. I really hate Allison.

Then, after a little time, things start to change again:

9. Perhaps she's changing a little, because she gave me her last piece of chocolate and a drink of her ginger beer last week.
8. Allison offered me a lift in her horsebox; she is really changing.

The circle goes round and round as your opinions change, but can you see it is you who are changing? Allison is in her own little world, unaffected by your torment. The moral of this story is that you can't change other people but you can change yourself, by catching yourself in the act of judging others and letting go. Then the mind becomes silent – remember the four-step programme.

Shaking Hands with Your Mind and Emotions

Once your mind becomes silent, your emotions also change.

> The sun shines on everything but rains bring a rainbow. They
> stream colour onto life. Clouds paint golden light in the sky, all that
> hardship you went through gave you strength.
>
> *P.R. Shankar*

In other words, don't always think of your suffering as a terrible thing, because it brings depth to you. You gain a much closer understanding and compassion with your fellow men and with your horse. Students who lack depth, who are more interested in using the horse to promote their own importance, never advance, as de la Guérinière points out:

> Yet swayed by the supposed good taste of the public, whose opinions are not always oracular and against which timid truth dare not
> revolt, find themselves having, after long and assiduous effort, nothing for their pains but the superficial and chimeric satisfaction of
> believing themselves more accomplished than others.

When we are suffering, we tend to look for company. If we see someone else in the midst of a problem, their downfall makes us feel comforted; gives us a confidence and strength from outside ourselves. We go in a cycle, a pattern; some problem comes and we feel down. Just turn back and look at your life: how many times have you had the same experience? Right from your childhood, recall what happened when you had a problem. You thought: 'This is the end, that's it.' Then it passed and some other problem came and, so on. But your world didn't end.

> Every rainy season in your life has made you ready for harvesting.
> Every rainy season has touched you deeply inside somewhere. It has
> made you grow. It has given you strength. It is never that rain is
> continuous; in one's life is there only the rainy season? No!
> Impossible! If someone thinks it is so, it is an illusion.
>
> *P.R. Shankar*

One weekend I was teaching a workshop just outside London and in the classroom stood an enormous rock of amethyst, almost a cubic yard in dimension. As we contemplated its age and shining beauty, it struck awe and wonder in us all. All except for one sceptical lady called Jane.

'For God's sake, what's all the fuss, it's only a piece of rock', she shouted. She sat as far away from it as possible, impatiently tapping the floor with her foot, a reminder to us that valuable workshop time was being wasted on 'airy-fairy-ness'. She had come for the meat, hard facts and theory, not sugar.

Astonished by her dryness I asked her if a baby is just a baby, or a miraculous happening of creation, just like the amethyst. She looked both dour and unconvinced, refusing to get more drawn in and thus waste even more time. She continued to be dry and cynical throughout most of the morning until we began the Darth Vader breathing.

I explained to the class that this ancient breathing technique is at least ten thousand years old, and is currently being revived and used in the West as a tool for stress management and for accessing deeper levels of ourselves, where old impressions (emotions) are stored in the body and nervous system. The breathing technique floods the body with prana (life energy, or chi), flushing out our negative emotions and toxins stored in every cell of the body. As the body detoxifies, so does the mind; thoughts subside to reveal to us our 'still point' inside. This is the seat of true learning, from where intuition comes.

We began the process, which involves closing the eyes and observing the mind. Ten minutes into the process, I was deeply touched to notice a little tear roll down Jane's cheek. When the process was finished I asked if anyone wanted to discuss their experiences. The colour of Jane's face had changed; it was as though she had shed an old skin and grown a new one. It looked almost translucent and flushed with colour. Jane was the third to speak.

'When you said it was an ancient yogic technique I was very sceptical, because I am a Christian.' I broke in there and explained that it is only a breathing technique, and actually you

> Ego weights you down.
> Your weight hurts others.
> One who is weightless is wise.
> A bird when it flies high,
> just floats. Float in life full
> of wisdom.

breathe like that naturally when you are asleep, whether you are Hindu, Christian, or Buddhist. What she said next was very beautiful.

'The process touched me deep inside; I felt as though I had come home after being lost in a hard, lonely place. Absorbed in my busy life, I had forgotten to save time for me.'

Later in the morning, I noticed that she had moved seats. She was now sitting directly in front of the amethyst, where she stayed for the rest of the day absorbing its healing energy. Her face was no longer dour; it was radiant, her eyes sparkled and a big smile beamed from ear to ear. She had come home and was rekindling her relationship with Creation.

When we touch the very rhythm of ourselves like Jane did: our existence; our very life; the very throbbing of our heart, that is our turning point, where we shift from getting stuck, singing the same old song.

To end this chapter I have included a poem by Alison Skeats, one of my assistant teachers; a contemplation on the wonderment of discovery:

February 20th 1996 – lunchtime ride on Sophie

I had one precious hour of riding time, and so much to work on. All morning I had been anticipating the thrill of progressing a new discovery in my riding technique and now the time had come and I had to be quick, fully utilise every second to maximise my riding time.

As I tacked up I became aware of unfriendly weather conditions. The wind was gale force; spooky objects were lurking in the hedge and grass, ready to launch themselves at us as we rode past – Sophie would not like this. Strange noises emanated from dark corners, scratchy branches on metal, hollow howling and whooshings. The roof was blowing off the shed in the next field. Gingerly, we paced round the school eyeing all the dangers. Sophie, becoming more and more agitated, started grinding the bit and nodding her head. Anxiety filled her complete being. Out of nowhere a helicopter swooped low, flying the hedge line only a hundred yards from our riding area. A huge well of resentment and frustration swept over me. I felt completely overwhelmed and helpless, trapped in the hands of my environment. My strong resolves of the morning had dissolved into nothingness . . .

Suddenly, the sun came out and the wind dropped for a minute – enough time to transform the fear and frustration into relief. A feeling of pure happiness grew from within as I felt the warmth of the sun and heard the birds singing. I began to sing – *The Sun Has Got His Hat On* – it seemed appropriate.

Drawing breath to sing lifted the rib hoops in my back; I sat properly on my seat bones, Sophie became light, a bird began to sing, everything was dazzling beauty – a blue sky, a glistening arena bedecked in a finery of sparkling jewels and crystals of snow. A cluster of huge tractors sat on the brow of a hill in the adjacent field, normally a threat, now magnificent and powerful, their paintwork shining and glowing against the backdrop of a thunderous sky. Wind blowing a cooling, refreshing breeze of ice-cold air over our bodies; Sophie's mane and tail streaming in elegant beauty. Again I sang; *Let's Go Fly a Kite* this time suited the mood, and concentrated on sending us both up to the dazzling sun, on swinging round with fire and sparkle, with activity and impulsion, actually going somewhere, dancing on the spot, skimming the arena, ballet dancing to the happy little tune, pretending to be the kite, soaring and sailing, flying on the wind. Behind us Shay Hill and Chell's willows were a backdrop of drama, dark and moody, swaying in the wind, while we were still highlighted in the sun, performing on stage. A thing of beauty and elegance.

Suddenly, the wind became a lot more forceful so that we had to plough into it, and a flurry of snow got up. The wind made each snowflake zoom around us and we merged into it using the energy of the wind to carry us round. Around each snowflake there was a lot of space and light and we were able to nip in and around the flakes still sailing and flying. Our minds were merged to the same tune. Agility and co-operation improved. All around us, the unfriendly weather conditions grew ever fiercer, but we didn't notice – we were having fun!

Congratulations on reading this chapter: now you really KNOW! knowing.

CHAPTER 12

SEMI-SUPINE: A RELAXATION TECHNIQUE

The rider's state of mind, emotions and character are all more important to horsemanship than are specific skills.

Charles de Kunffy

In our busy daily life it is so easy to forget ourselves, as Jane did in Chapter 11. We tend to forget about our bodies until they shout at us in pain. Most of our busy day is spent thinking and talking. Usually, we are sitting in front of a computer or at a desk, for hour after hour. We tend to overuse our mind and underuse our body. The root of all tension lies in the mind and resting the body is a great way to rest and quieten the tape in our head.

The semi-supine relaxation technique (Figure 19) coupled with Darth Vader breathing will take care of mind/body imbalance. You may think you haven't got time: that is what many people say, but aren't you worth it? Think how much time you spend watching television. By practising the technique your nervous system will be soothed and you will finish the lesson feeling rejuvenated. If you feel bored or fidgety it is usually a sign that you are stressed, so just build up five minutes at a time each day. It takes eighteen minutes for the discs between your vertebrae to fill up with fluid after being compressed and flattened as a result of you being vertical all day. If you find you are falling asleep whilst employing the semi-supine exercise you are overtired, and should think of getting more early nights. Try to get into the habit of using the semi-supine technique on a daily basis; even if it's only for ten minutes you will reap the benefits, not only in your riding but also in your daily life. It rejuvenates the spine, is a good pick-me-up, and educates your body into the primary control.

During this exercise, allow your mind to contact parts of the body very effortlessly, so that there is no mental strain. Allow your mind to contact your body in a very effortless, easy way and allow your body to respond. Please don't make any physical effort, for example, to push the small of your back onto the floor. Allow your awareness to effortlessly explore and meet your body. Until you are familiar with the process, it may help to have a friend or partner read it out to you.

Lie down in the position shown in Figure 19, with the books under your head. Allow your spine to enjoy the support of the floor. Keep your feet and knees hip-distance apart, knees pointing to the ceiling, heels about 30 cm (1 ft) from your buttocks. Have your hands resting palms down on the lower abdomen.

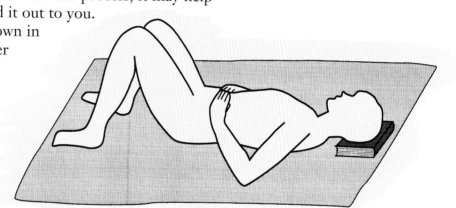

Figure 19
The semi-supine
relaxation technique.

Next, close your eyes. Feel the contact of your head on the books. Imagine you have been holding your head up off the books and now you are going to let it go. Think of your head as light and empty.

Relax the back of your neck. Imagine that someone has placed a warm pad there. Your neck is dropping down and relaxing into the warm pad. Now take your attention to your forehead. Think of a soothing, warm pad releasing all the tensions. Take your attention to your right eye: relax your eye, then do the same with your left eye.

Now take your awareness to the space in between your eyebrows. We tend to tighten this area through trying too hard. So now just let go. Let this area spread and have space. Notice the air going in and out of your nostrils spontaneously as you breathe.

Take your attention to your right cheekbone; your left cheekbone; the roof of your mouth. Think of your mouth as hollow and empty. Take your attention to your tongue and the back of your throat. Make sure you are not clenching your teeth.

Take your attention to the space in between your ears and behind your nose, in the inner depth of your head. This is where the head fits onto the spine. I will refer to this place as the mid-point. Relax this area and notice any effect this has on your neck.

Take your attention to your breastbone. That's the bone in the centre of the chest that starts at the base of the throat and goes down to where the right and left parts of the rib-cage separate. Imagine that a warm pad has been placed on the breastbone. Allow it to lengthen and widen, and notice it move spontaneously as you breathe.

Take your attention to the right side of your rib-cage. Feel your spine resting on the floor. Think of giving more space in between your ribs on this side as you take in deep breaths. Release your right armpit. Imagine you have been holding the right side of your rib-cage up off the floor, and now you are going to let it go. Now repeat for the left side of the rib-cage.

Become aware of your shoulder-blades resting on the floor. The shoulder-blades are movable, not fixed. Be aware that your upper torso is resting down onto your shoulder-blades. Imagine that you have been holding your shoulder-blades up, and now you are going to let them go.

Take your attention to your right elbow, then wrist. Think of the wrist as light and empty. Watch your wrist absorb the movement of your body as your hand goes up and down with your breath, just as you absorb the movement of the horse when you ride. You need to be this free. Then repeat with your left arm.

Take your attention to your navel/stomach area. Notice and welcome any sensations without judging them to be bad or good. Let the weight of your stomach fall back into your lower ribs and through the floor. Allow a smile to come onto your face. Transfer the sensation of smiling to your stomach/navel area. Gently smile across your stomach.

Smile across your chest. Imagine you have been holding your upper back up off the floor, and now you are going to let it go.

Take your attention to your lower belly/pelvis area. Notice and welcome any sensations. Think of gently smiling across the

> If your desires keep changing, know that you are growing. Otherwise, you remain stagnant.

lower belly. Imagine you have been holding your lower back up off the floor, and now you are going to let it go. Can you let go of the back of your waist any more?

Take your attention to your right hip. Think of your right hip as light and empty. Move on to your left hip. Imagine you have been holding your hips up off the floor, and now you are going to let them go.

Relax your right kneecap. Think of it drifting up to the ceiling. While the knee is drifting up, allow the weight of the leg to drop down into the hip and foot, leaving the kneecap light. Then repeat with the left kneecap. Imagine a little string on the kneecap with a little pulley delicately easing the kneecap up to the ceiling and, as it eases up, the weight of your leg drops into the left hip and left foot.

Take your attention to your pelvic floor, to all the genital area. It is very important for you as a rider to relax this area so that you don't become perched on your saddle.

Next, take your attention to the toes of your right foot. Think of them growing away from the heel, out into the space in front of them as the arch of the foot releases.

Then add the left side. Think of both kneecaps drifting up to the ceiling as your heels grow down through the floor; the arches of your feet relax; the balls of your feet relax; your toes spread on the floor. Let the soles of your feet enjoy the floor. Have a sense of your soles yawning and spreading.

Now take your attention to the top of your head, right in the middle. Be aware of the space from the middle of your head to 30 cm (1 ft) out towards the wall . . . and now further out into the room . . . to the wall . . . and now beyond the wall into the fields, up through the trees, into the clouds, towards the sun. Beyond the sun to the cosmos. In this peaceful space full of stars, find yourself a star. Let the crown of your head connect with the star.

And now return back, down through the clouds, back into the world, into the treetops, into the fields, back into the room. Be aware of your surroundings.

Now take your attention to your coccyx, a tiny bone at the end of your spine. Move to the top of your head. Think of your spine in between as hollow and empty. Think of the coccyx and head growing away from each other. Think once more of your star and, without moving, think of your head easing forwards and up towards your star. Let the rest of your body hang down on the floor. Notice the sensation of your head going forwards and up.

This is the end of this guided visualization. Slowly open your eyes, and before you move, orientate yourself again in the room. Roll over gradually onto your side, keeping your neck free, to come up into standing.

COMPARING PARTS

Every action generates a force of energy that returns to us in like kind . . . what we sow is what we reap. And when we choose actions that bring happiness and success to others, the fruit of our karma is happiness and success.

Deepak Chopra

In spite of their size, horses are incredibly sensitive creatures. If you consider how they react when a fly lands on their side, you can imagine how every tiny movement you make affects them! Take, for example, breathing in and out: become aware of your breathing, now take a big, long breath in through your nose, and notice how your spine extends as you inhale. Are your head and neck fixing back and down? Then feel your spine release and flex as you exhale. Can you see how, by holding your breath, you can fix yourself and block the absorption of the horse's movement through your spine?

Often, riders breathe in a shallow fashion from the top of the chest, underusing their internal athletic ability. The horse follows suit by shortening his back and his stride, or by hurrying. How many times does this happen when you are competing, worried, or end-gaining. Many riders I meet confess that they hold their breath while competing, never fully realising the ramifications of this on their performance! However, animals only hold their breath as a reflex action if they are startled by something. So when a horse feels the rhythm of your breathing suddenly change or stop, he assumes that you're worried and he should be too!

When you allow air deep into your body in regular Darth Vader breaths (see Chapter 9), the horse starts to relax as he

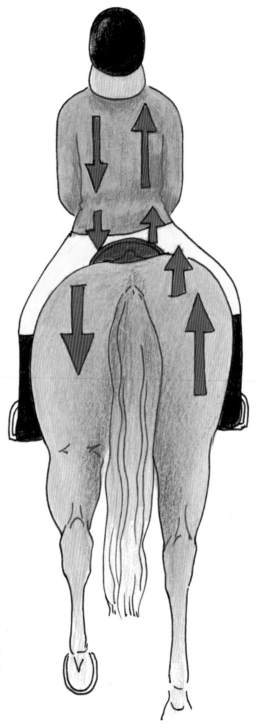

Figure 20
Deepening your seat. As the
horse's body swings from side
to side, absorb the lowering
of his barrel by growing up
through your ribs. Allow your
legs to hang and lengthen as
your seat deepens. Be careful
not to anticipate the movement:
if you try to drop your legs when
you 'think' the belly would swing
under, you could interfere with
his natural rhythm. Remember,
'feel', don't 'anticipate'.

begins to feel your calming, rhythmic breathing. Your improved breathing also improves your balance and deepens your seat so your horse reaps all these benefits. Because your whole body has relaxed, you become more coherent and give better aids; the horse responds likewise, and that adds brilliance to your performance.

Exercise: deepening your seat

When the horse's left hind leg steps forward, his belly swings to the right, and his right hind leg supports his weight. As his right hind leg steps forward his belly swings left, and so on. Darth Vader breathing gives more support to your upper body: absorb the horse's movements up through your upper body on the inhale and exhale. At the same time, the more your lower body releases and follows the horse's movement with soft, allowing (as opposed to hard, driving) legs, the more freely the horse's back can work, and his quarters engage (see Figure 20).

Tension

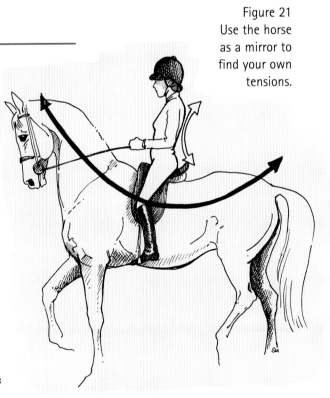

Figure 21
Use the horse as a mirror to find your own tensions.

Besides reacting to changes in your breathing the horse will also react to subtle increases of muscle tension. Take eyes for example. Hard, narrowly focused eyes, that fix on one spot such as the horse's poll, start a chain reaction of stiffness going through the bodies of both you and your horse (see Figure 21). Although you are staring at the horse's poll you are actually still looking inwards. The easiest way to soften your eyes and open up is to drop the blinds on the back of your eyeballs and be master of all you survey, totally looking out.

Use your horse to mirror your own tensions, because spotting them in yourself can be hard. He will show you where you are tense – observe his tensions with the help of a friend and compare that place in yourself (see Figure 22). He may be hollow; are you? He may be above the bit; are you?

Figure 22
Hard, narrowly focused eyes, that fix on one spot such as the horse's poll, start a chain reaction of stiffness going through the bodies of both you and the horse. Although you are staring at the horse's poll you are actually still looking inwards. The easiest way to soften your eyes is to drop the 'blinds' on the back of your eyeballs and be master of all you survey, totally looking out.

His action may be stiff; is yours? Are you locking your hips, instead of allowing them to move freely with his motion? If so, you'll limit the freedom of swing in *his* hips.

One-sidedness

Check your own one-sidedness by observing the horse's. Does he go better in one direction than the other? Does his back feel lower on one side than the other? Instead of spending hours doing gymnastic bending exercises to try to even him up – as conventional training teaches us – look deeper into the way you are using your own body – and that means first checking your own evenness! It doesn't make sense to practise endless school movements incorrectly if you are riding on one side of his back more than the other. Just think how a hiker would look and feel on returning from a walk if you had loaded his rucksack mainly on the right side (see Figure 23). Besides being pretty annoyed he'd certainly look and feel lop-sided – and he'd have backache, to boot. During his walk the uneven loading would force him to carry more weight on his right leg, 'leaking out' of his right ribs and hollow in his left ribs. This is what you do when you sit too far to the right, loading that stirrup more than the left and then wondering why it always feels shorter.

As mentioned in Chapter 4 Does Right Feel Right, because of right-sidedness your body eventually starts to favour that side and, like a horse, you become hollow on the left (see Photo 16). So when riding on the right rein, moving the rib-cage over to the left proves difficult for most riders. This is because the left ribs are used to being set close together: because that side

Photo 16
Because of right-sidedness, your body eventually starts to favour that side.

Figure 23   Think how a hiker would look and feel on returning from a walk if you had loaded his rucksack
mainly on the right side.

is less used to being worked it is more prone to hollowing. On the other hand the right ribs – the soft side – are the opposite, over-stretched in comparison. What makes things more difficult is that the horse is usually also hollow on the left and soft on the right – we actively encourage this by mounting, leading, etc. from the left! Through turns and circles you must proficiently perform in yourself what you are asking of your horse. In other words, your left and right sides must be equal in their dexterity. This is the foundation of straightness which many people lack. I often find that by getting riders into the left side of their body, they suddenly slip much deeper and sit more around the horse, so don't be surprised if this happens to you.

The smoothness and rhythm of your horse's paces will improve noticeably when you free yourself up with the exercises in this chapter. As your evenness increases your stiffness releases – and guess who also frees up and straightens!

Seat Bones

Focus your attention on the details of what is happening under your seat bones as your horse swings each hind leg forward, shifts his weight onto it and steps under himself with the other hind leg. The more his back and hind legs are allowed to work, the more your seat bones rise and fall. If a part of you is stiff and not following the movement, you will block the corresponding part in his anatomy.

Now, with you sitting on the deepest, lowest part of your seat bones we will look more closely at their movement. First of all I'd like you to check that they are moving separately up and down. The greater the degree of collection in the horse's back, the less the seat bones will move. Because we are only riding the horse in a novice outline right now, there will be a lot of movement in walk, so give your body completely to the horse and absorb his movement. Give yourself time to really *feel*. Watch out for *the driving seat* (see Photos 17 and 18). Driving seat bones *can* be very subtle but, in what is termed the 'driving seat', the seat bones do not work unilaterally, but are held tight together – bio-laterally – 'polishing' the saddle from the cantle

Photo 17–18
Two examples of the 'driving seat'.

to the pommel. They *should* be moving up and down separately on either side of the horse's spine, not forwards and backwards sticking together. Do you get a feeling that your hips and seat bones are softly describing circles as the horse is walking along? My students find that thinking of their seat bones and hips as little watermills, paddling forwards with the horse's motion up, over and forward towards his shoulders, helps the horse's movement to flow more. When they want to slow down, they imagine that the wheels are paddling backwards towards his hocks. Remember, it's a releasing thought, not a forced action. Be careful not to anticipate the movement. Listen and feel, don't think!

If your seat bones are travelling with the horse's back, they will move in three sets of directions: up/down; forward/backward; and sideways (see Figure 24). Can you feel the three

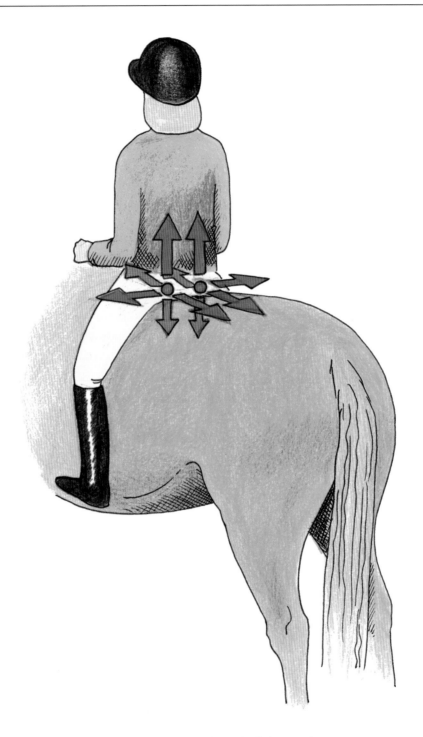

Figure 24   The three planes of travel of the seat bones.

planes of movement as the horse's hind legs step under and his shoulders stretch out? When the right hind leg engages and pushes off it will lift your right seat bone, and the same with the left. Are you more aware of one of your seat bones than the other?

Riding 'Side by Side'

To make a circle, the horse has to stretch the outside of his body in a much bigger arc than the inside (see Figure 25). In essence you must mirror this in your own body although without hollowing on the inside. Keep balanced over both seat bones to keep the horse balanced evenly over his hind legs. Use the following exercises to become 'equal on both reins'.

Exercise: establishing the habitual way you use yourself
First, whilst mounted, notice your seat bones being moved by the horse as he walks along. Then notice your rib-cage moving in relation to them. Keep changing the rein and notice how you carry your upper body on each rein. Ask a friend for feedback. After a little while you will observe your habitual patterns. Find out which is your hollow side and which side you 'leak out' of – this is your soft side. Having established your hollow and soft sides, you are now more clued up as to your crookedness. Keep this in mind during the following exercise.

If you hollow your inside rib-cage too much, like the hiker with the uneven rucksack, both you and the horse will drift out through your soft side. To prevent this, put your hands in the air while practising. Allow your hips to grow down as you grow up. (Remember to keep growing up through your upper body when you put your hands back down.) On the left rein, if you are right-handed, you will probably find that you 'leak out' of your right ribs and slip out to the right (see Figure 26). To correct this on this rein sit to the inside and stabilise your outside ribs by keeping stretched up through them, up through your fingertips to the sky. Release your left hip and leg down to the earth. Check that your head is releasing up, not propping sideways.

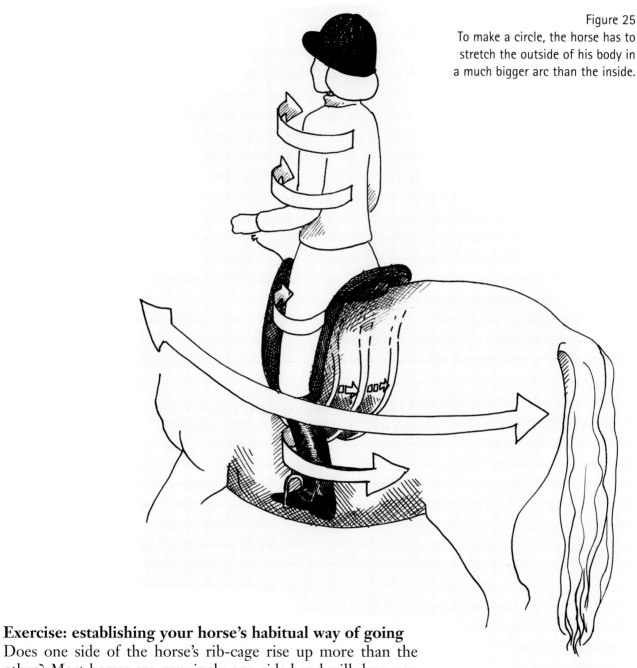

Figure 25
To make a circle, the horse has to stretch the outside of his body in a much bigger arc than the inside.

Exercise: establishing your horse's habitual way of going
Does one side of the horse's rib-cage rise up more than the other? Most horses are genuinely one-sided and will drop you down more to one side. You will have to make allowances for that when you place yourself on the horse. For example, if he drops you down to the right more than the left this means his

Figure 26
Correction for 'leaking out' through
the right ribs. Sit to the inside,
stabilise your outside ribs by keeping
stretched up through your inside ribs
and releasing your left hip and leg
down to earth.

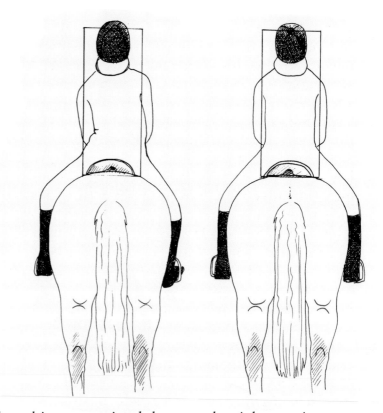

barrel is more twisted down to the right, putting more weight
and strain on the right hock. To balance him you will have to
really 'get into' the left side of your body and sit more to the left
until his body changes, allowing you to sit centrally. Ask a friend
to stand in a corner of the school and watch you travel up the
long side on the left rein. (You could also place a camcorder
there.) Is the horse making you hollow your left rib, like the
crooked hiker? If he is, keep stretching your left foot down to
the ground while stretching your fingertips up to the sky. Keep
your ribs stretched over to the left and really stretch until the
hollowing disappears. Stabilising your left side in this way eventually straightens the horse, as he will mirror you. When you
put your hand down ask your friend to check that you are main-
taining the stability in your left side. Now think of creating a
bigger distance between the bone protruding just under your
left ear, your left seat bone and left foot. Keep your right side
straight. Notice whether you are allowing the horse's motion to
travel up through one side of your torso more than the other. If

you find this is the case, then you are more fixed and therefore blocking the horse on the side that is not moving. You must receive and absorb the horse's motion as it rises and falls through your torso equally.

Exercise: turning
Raise both arms and allow your outside rib-cage to elongate a little to allow for the horse's outside bend keeping you both 'side by side'. Don't forget to keep stretching up through your inside rib-cage to prevent it from hollowing. As you stretch your outside thigh off and back you must keep it spiralled inward so that the outside seat bone stays out, back and down, well clear of the horse's spine. While the outside leg is stretching back and down, the pelvis and torso on the same side spiral around, independently, following the horse around the turn. It is essential that your upper body is stretched up and over your outside seat bone at the same time (see Figure 26). If you tip your upper body in, the horse will tip and fall in. Using the outside hip and leg in this way allows more room for the horse's outside bend. The pelvis and upper body ease the horse around the turn. By stretching your outside leg back and down towards the horse's outside hind foot you not only prevent the horse's quarters from swinging out, you also keep his back level. Without your outside thigh anchoring his outside ribs down, his barrel would be prone to tip to the inside on a turn. If the horse's back is not kept level through turns and circles you will not be able to ride deeply into the corners; your turn will be more of a tip.

When you don't take your outside thigh off and back, or you allow it to slip forwards, you lose the inward spiral of the thigh, the outside seat bone moves diagonally in towards the horse's spine and your outside hip collapses, giving you an incorrect bend. The inside seat bone and leg must be in advance of the outside, not only to make a channel for the horse to bend around, but also in order that he understands in which direction to go from the placement of your seat.

To develop the downward and backward stretch of the outside leg more, and to increase the flexibility and action of the ankles and knees as springs and shock-absorbers, you must be

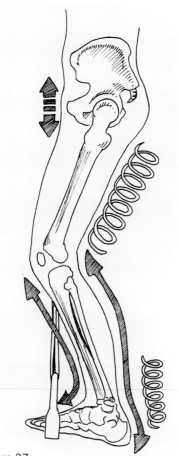

Figure 27
Release the front of the ankles and
continue that release up to
the kneecaps.

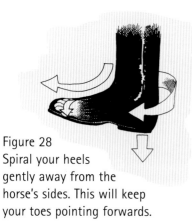

Figure 28
Spiral your heels
gently away from the
horse's sides. This will keep
your toes pointing forwards.

able to release them. Often riders don't, or can't. As you may recall from Chapter 10, my inability to flex in these joints resulted in my perched seat, severely limiting my range of movement and flexibility.

Exercise: releasing the lower leg

Release the front of the ankles and continue that release up to the kneecaps (see Figure 27). Then release the backs of the knees and allow that release to continue down into the calf muscles; to the backs of the ankles; through the heel bones, and down to the floor. Keep the inward spiral started at the thighs going all the way down to the feet. Spiral your heels gently away from the horse's sides: this will keep your toes pointing forwards (see Figure 28). Position the stirrups under the balls of your feet, not under the toes or too close to the heels. The heel can then drop softly downward, allowing the ankle joint to flex freely with the horse's movement. The heels then sink below the level of the toes giving an effective, stable position and putting impulsion (oomph) behind your riding.

Exercise: increasing the absorption of the horse's movement through your upper body

Lightening your upper body lifts and lightens the horse's carriage. Hold your left arm up vertically then bend the elbow, placing the palm of your hand in the space between your shoulder-blades (see Figure 29). Keep your fingers straight. Work your elbow up until your ribs are stretched to their full extent and your armpit is wide open, then add the right arm. Imagine that your arms and rib-cage are like big wings opening and stretching forwards, up and out to their full extent. Allow your stomach to stretch. Next, straighten your arms up vertically, palms facing inwards, fingertips stretching up to the sky, little finger slightly in advance. Find out if one side of your rib-cage is more stuck than the other and work more on that side. Stretch it out and even up your torso.

Once again, with your elbows up and palms between your shoulder-blades, make some turns, allowing the outside of your torso to stretch up and out over your outside seat bone, without lifting your shoulders or hollowing yourself on the inside.

Figure 29   Imagine that your arms and rib-cage are like big wings opening and stretching forwards, up and out to their full extent.

Separate at the hip and slightly spiral in the direction of movement. As the outside hip drops, keep your outside leg stretched back and down, with a gentle inward spiral to the horse's outside hind leg. Change the rein and repeat. Notice the stretch in your abdominal muscles from your pubic arch right up to your breastbone. Let these muscles be long and wide. Then lengthen down the back of your spine right down to your tail-bone, through the horse's belly to the ground, freeing your lower back.

By allowing your rib-cage to stretch up and out of your pelvis you release your lower back and it can then oscillate freely with the movement of the horse. (Most riders fix down, stiffening in their upper body. How can your lower back and pelvis oscillate freely under this great downward pressure?)

Points to remember
- The easiest way to soften your eyes and open up is to drop the 'blinds' on the back of your eyeballs. Be master of all you survey, totally looking out.
- Right-handed riders are prone to 'leak out' of their ribs and slip to the right. On the right rein, ask a friend to check from behind that you are not slipping to the inside, hollowing on the left. On the left rein ask them to check the same thing. Your torso and hips must be square over the horse's back, as he will mirror you. Starting to use your left ribs will feel strange at first, as though you are falling off to the left, so don't be put off by 'faulty sensory appreciation'.
- Deepen your seat with the Darth Vader breathing.
- Your seat bones travel and mirror the movement of the horse's hind legs. They should move alternately and unilaterally; not stuck together as in a 'driving seat'.
- Keep an opposing stretch on turns: as your upper body gently describes the circle your leg stretches back and down in the opposite direction to stabilise the horse's rib-cage and hindquarters.
- Grow up and out of your pelvis to free your lower back and allow it to oscilliate with the horse's movement.
- Lighten your carriage with the elbow exercise. Keep stretched up through your upper body; absorb the alternate drop of the horse's barrel up through your sides.

THREE SEATS OF INSTRUCTION

Many people assume that the manner of training war and hunting horses is quite different from the rules of the manège. So poorly founded an idea is, also, only too widespread, and neglects the true principles of horsemanship.

de la Guérinière

The classical dressage seat is the foundation for all disciplines of equitation. The light seat and the jumping seat should not be viewed as distinct from the dressage seat, but as adaptations of it, made for specific purposes.

The Dressage Seat

The classical riding position as we know it today is a result of the natural evolution of great knowledge and experience. It can be traced back to the Greek general, Xenophon over two thousand years ago. The aim of the rider is to follow smoothly the movements of the horse's back, keeping his own centre above that of the horse.

Riding with good posture improves the rider's performance in the saddle by creating freer absorption of the horse's movement and allowing more powerful and finer-tuned aids, which direct the horse without hindering his natural grace and beauty. Slumping, straining, tightening and forcing interfere with the horse's natural flow. It takes great skill to maintain a good, effective posture, while, at the same time, remaining in balance with the horse as he moves.

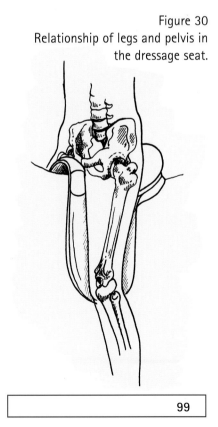

Figure 30
Relationship of legs and pelvis in the dressage seat.

99

Horses rely for direction on the signals given throughout the rider's body. Therefore, as we saw in Part One, we need self-mastery in order to achieve horse-mastery. If this self-mastery is achieved, with the rider's body being used well, the rider will be open to 'feel' and the aids will be reliable and coherent, allowing the full potential of the partnership to be realised.

Before discussing the correct dressage seat in more detail, it may be useful to look at two incorrect versions; the 'chair' seat and the 'fork' seat.

The Chair Seat

Xenophon recognised that the rider should not sit as though sitting on a chair, but rather as if standing, legs apart. This is because the chair seat puts the rider behind the movement and hinders the horse's free forward movement. Not only does the horse feel as though someone had left the handbrake half on, this posture also prevents correct use of the aids. When the upper body is placed behind the vertical, the legs have to grip forwards and upwards to prevent the rider from falling off backwards. If the legs are not underneath the rider's body, they cannot be used to bend the horse in the correct place, or to keep him straight. The rider loses control of the horse's shoulders, and has to rely on the reins for steering, creating over-bending in the neck, blocking of the shoulders, and loss of control over the hindquarters.

Correcting the Chair Seat

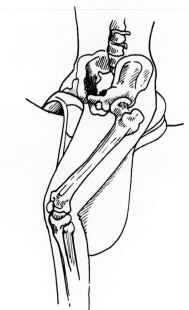

Figure 31
Relationship of legs and pelvis in the chair seat.

Here I would like to introduce you to Lynne, who kindly permitted me to use the photographs taken of herself and her horse, Taurean, in their first assessment lesson with me. I have used them throughout this book to give you an idea of how the Alexander technique can help people like Lynne, who haven't had any Alexander lessons before, rather than using pictures of someone more established. I decided to do this to put the record straight. I hear it bandied about the horse world that the Alexander technique is OK, but it's very slow and it just improves the rider's posture – as if that were not very important

Photo 19 The author's pupil, Lynn and her horse,
Taurean.

Photo 20 Typical chair seat.

in training a horse! A little knowledge is a dangerous thing, and
such ill-informed comment can put enthusiastic people off. The
technique is certainly not slow: in my opinion slow progress
comes to riders with a sloppy, incorrect seat and a closed, end-
gaining mind.

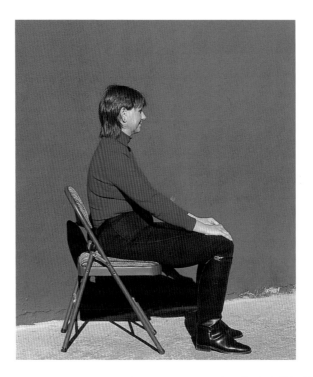

Photo 21
How Lynne sits in chair.

Photo 22
Using the elbow
exercise to cure
frontal slouch.

Photo 23
Sitting on the low-
est central part of
the seat bones.

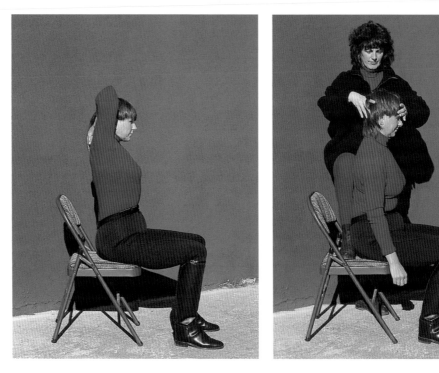

To correct the chair seat, you must first observe how you are sitting when dismounted. Photo 21 shows how Lynne sits in a chair. She works in an office, spending hour after hour in front of a computer. Because she has long legs and most chairs aren't high enough for her (like the one in the picture), she is caused to slouch and close down the front of her body. To help remedy this I gave her the elbow exercise (Photo 22) which is something she can do for herself to open up the front of her body. After this, I placed her more on the lowest central part of her seat bones (Photo 23).

Usually, when riders try to correct a chair seat, they force their legs back and under themselves. However, if the upper body is not balanced directly above the lowest central part of the seat bones, the rider will have a battle on their hands (Photo 24). This is because the legs are part of a whole unit – legs, pelvis, spine, neck and head, and must be treated as such. In Photo 25 Lynne's knee looks too deep but as she takes back her stirrup and her back lengthens and widens with Alexander lessons, the leg, pelvis, spine, neck and head unit will work more harmoniously and she will develop a powerful, correct classical seat.

Photo 24–25
Working on correcting the
chair seat.

Figure 32
The fork seat.

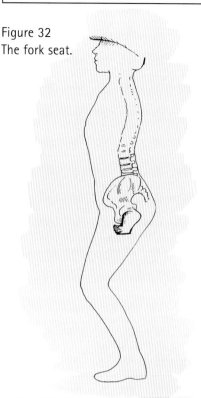

Photo 26   Lynne posing a fork seat.

How not to Correct a Chair Seat

It really takes some conscious thought to cure a chair seat successfully. What happens if you don't correct the upper body first, before taking the thigh off and back? The legs won't be able to release down or be spiralled in successfully because the legs only release properly as a result of the head, neck and upper body moving forwards, up and out of the pelvis. Without this, not only will the legs keep creeping forwards; the seat bones will slip in diagonally towards the horse's spine and the backs of the thighs will begin to grip up. The knees will creep up and forwards and the rider will be back at square one, on the back of the thighs, behind the movement, in a chair seat.

The Fork Seat

I would echo Charles de Kunffy's thoughts on the fork seat:

'That horrible position nullifies the functions of the lower back, which, in my opinion, is where riding is! Riders who press the crotch down, pushing the hips ahead of the seat bones, and slant the lower abdomen over the pommel, have never felt what riding is'.

I asked Lynn to sit in a fork seat (Photo 26) in order to experience the opposite extreme from a chair seat. Most riders with this fault sit too far up the cantle with their seat bones sticking out behind them. If you have this problem, place your thighs on the front of the saddle to move you nearer to the pommel (Photo 27). When you have moved further forwards in the saddle, take your legs off it and back – make sure that you don't stick your tail-bone and seat bones up and out behind

Photo 27
Placing the thighs on the front of the saddle to move nearer to the pommel.

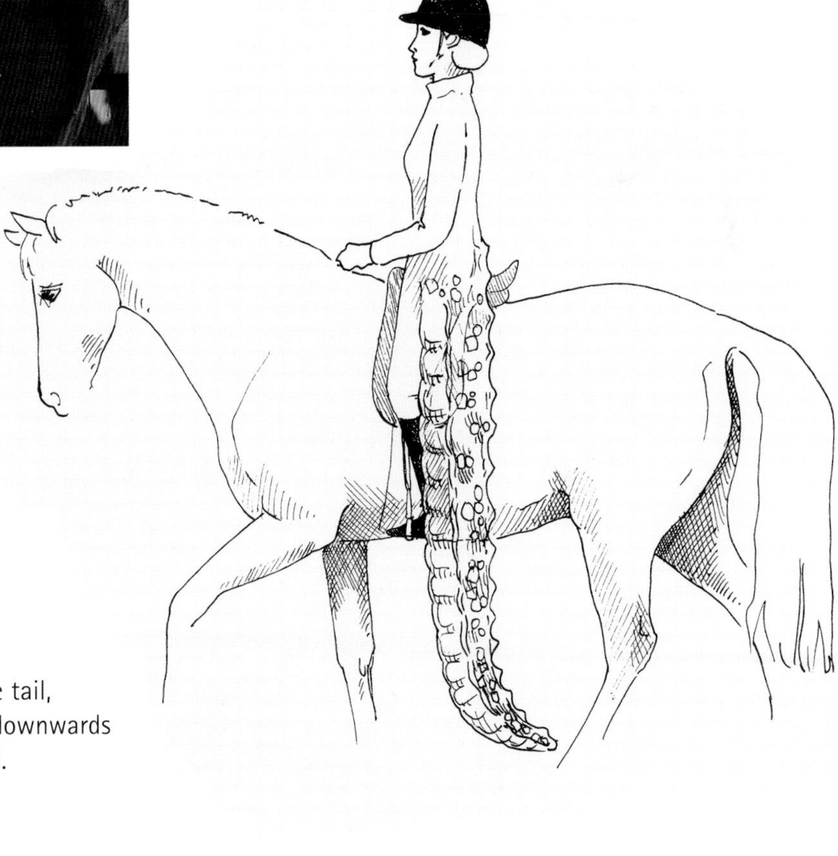

you, tilting your pelvis forwards again. Imagine that you have a heavy crocodile tail, which is keeping your sacrum pointing downwards through the horse's belly to the ground (see Figure 33). Initially, you may feel like the proverbial 'sack of spuds', but this is a consequence of faulty sensory appreciation (see Chapter 4), and will soon pass. (Likewise, a rider who has been sitting in a chair seat may feel, on coming more upright, that they are falling forwards. However, the change of position will soon start to feel more natural, and reverting to the old way will feel terrible.)

Figure 33
Imagine that you have a heavy crocodile tail, which is keeping your sacrum pointing downwards through your horse's belly to the ground.

Spice up Your Dressage Seat with the Alexander Technique

Developing the primary control creates optimum use of your body, putting you into 'self-carriage'; keeping you straight and free from tension. This also allows your horse optimum use of his body. Releasing the lower body and heels downward keeps your seat deep and propels the horse forward, while the upward stretch increases the lightness and spring in the horse's step. Your 'self-carriage' allows the lower body more freedom to absorb the horse's movement fully. You can then be said to be working 'through', building up the 'oomph' required for maximum impulsion. The aim of dressage is more '*schwung*', which enables the horse to move in the most expressive way that nature gave him. Opposing stretch gives similar '*schwung*' to the rider. To experience this reliably, you will need to take yourself off to an Alexander teacher.

Suppling the spine

I placed Lynn, dismounted, on the correct part of her seatbones and gave her a little taste of an Alexander lesson (see Photo 28). Then I gently mobilised her spine with my fingertips to help her understand how it oscillates – arches and releases – from head to tail as it absorbs the horse's movement (Photo 29).

Although you can't give each other actual Alexander lessons without being qualified Alexander teachers, you can improve the absorption of the horse's movement through your spine using the following exercises:

1. While your friend gently oscillates your spine, place your elbows vertically skyward, armpits wide open (Photo 22, p102). Don't collapse too much on the release and thus slouch. Keep yourself poised but soft, keeping your attention up and out into the world. Your friend should begin to work slowly up your spine, one vertebra at a time, from your tail-

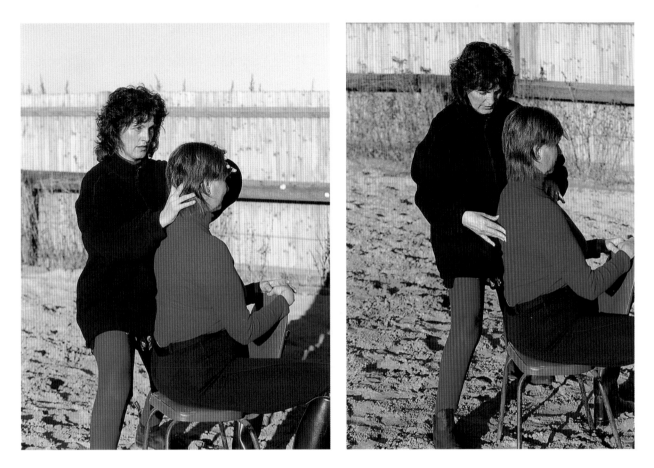

Photo 28–29   An Alexander lesson dismounted.

Photo 28   Placing the pupil on the correct part of   Photo 29 Mobilising the spine.
the seat bones.

bone. Mobilising your spine in this way helps to work on releasing any 'sticking' bits. If you have been sitting in a fork seat, ask your friend to support your tail-bone with their spare hand, easing it downward so that your pelvis doesn't tip forwards. Check that your jaw is released and soft. As your back arches inwards, allow yourself to make a inhaling, gasping sound: as it releases, breathe out. The breathing allows the oscillation to happen more freely and releases knotted-up tension deep down in your abdomen and stomach.

2. Now mounted, in walk, rather than your friend oscillating your spine, allow the horse to do it. Pay special attention to your sacral area. Riders are often blocked here through trying too hard and driving with the seat. Make sure it is being softly oscillated and absorbing the horse's movement – you may need to mobilise it with your fingertips. Then work your way to the top of the spine, giving attention to the area in between the shoulder-blades, often blocked by backward-pulling hands and slouching. If your attention is coming up and out into the world, while your heavy 'crocodile tail' and seat bones release down to the ground, your position will eventually become proud and elegant.

To be straight when in motion you must be:

1. 'Going forwards' in the movement, with your attention lively and leading.
2. 'Equal on both reins'; weight distributed equally over the horse's back.
3. 'On the bit'; head leading the movement from a relaxed, but toned neck and spine, the spine employing its optimum length and strength to absorb and direct the horse's movement.

When this 'way of going' is established, the rider can appreciate the parallels between themselves and any movement they want from the horse. They will see that the movement starts with themselves first, and this gives a true understanding of what they are asking of the horse, springing from a true understanding of their own experience. Riding requires of the rider the same degree of attentiveness, suppleness and self-carriage that is required of the horse; only then can the horse respond happily and generously.

The Light Seat

This is used for flatwork, show jumping, gymnastic jumping, hacking, cross-country, backing and training a young horse and retraining and strengthening horses with weak, hollow backs.

The light seat combines security with lightness and, over rough terrain, the rider can stay in balance more easily.

The stirrups are adjusted about two holes shorter than for dressage. The rider folds the upper body forwards, in one piece, from the hip joints until it is slightly in front of the vertical. This seat lessens the pressure of the seat bones in the saddle, because the rider can now carry more weight on the thighs.

In this seat, it is important that your lower legs do not slip back-

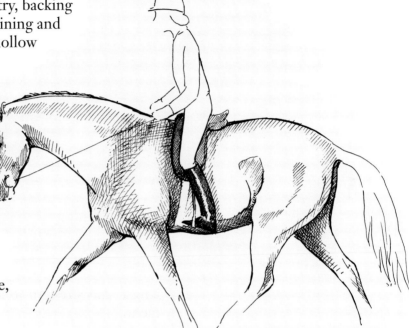

Figure 34   The light seat.

wards. The pelvis must follow the horse's movement with suppleness, and the hips, knees and ankles must act as springs to absorb your weight with every stride.

The Jumping Seat

Work on this only when you have developed a good dressage seat and light seat. The jumping seat is designed to give freedom for the bascule and to enable the rider to mirror swiftly all the changes in the horse's balance.

When jumping, this seat is used only over a fence, the light seat being used in between fences. The stirrup leathers should be adjusted quite short, depending on the rider's physique.

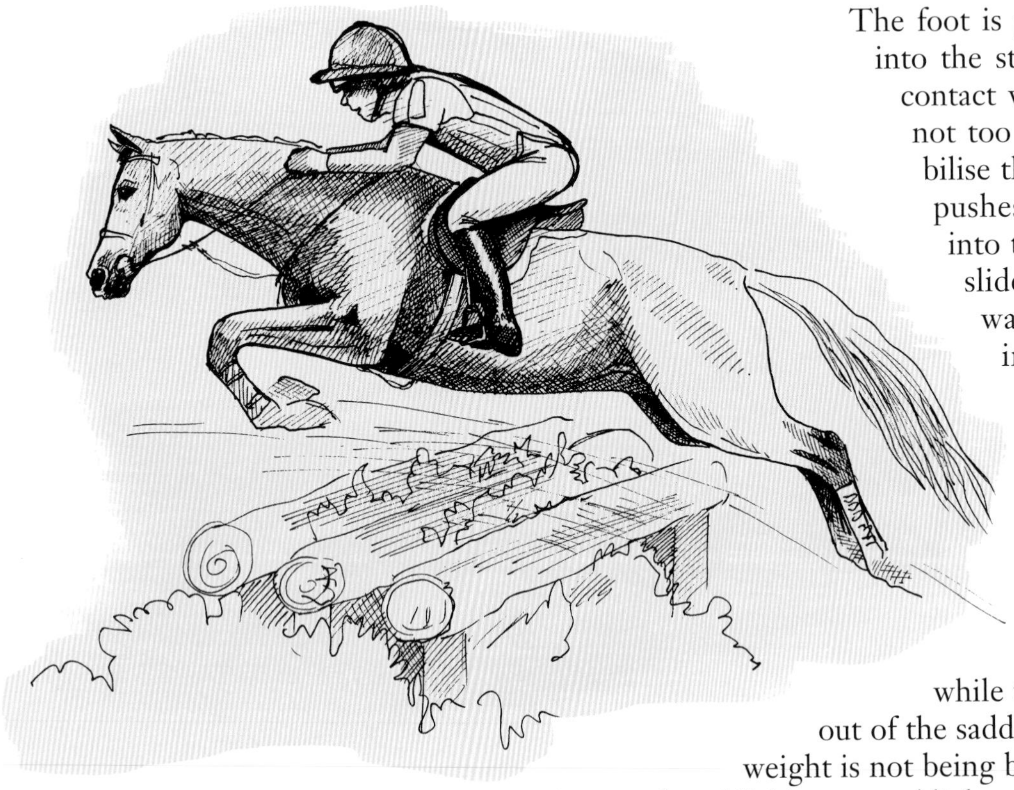

Figure 35   The jumping seat.

The foot is pushed slightly further into the stirrup to keep a firmer contact with the lower leg, but not too far, as this will immobilise the ankle joint. The calf pushes the horse forwards into the contact; it must not slide backwards and forwards, because this inhibits the horse's movement and makes the rider unstable. The upper body is folded more in front of the vertical than with the light seat. Hips and knee joints should remain elastic, while the seat is lifted slightly out of the saddle so that it is close, but weight is not being borne on the seat bones.

The art of establishing a good light seat or jumping seat is to allow yourself to grow back and down from the waist towards the horse's hind feet, directing your tail and seat bones back and down while your upper body grows up and out. Imagine that you are like an egg timer: all the sand has transferred from your upper body into your lower body, flooding into the backs of your legs and ankles and weighing heavily towards the floor around your horse's hind feet. This brings stability to your position. Use this image to improve your opposing stretch.

In summary, for a light or jumping seat, work on developing:

1. Deep heels and knees.
2. Steady hands, held low on both sides of the horse's wither: the feeling of the horse cantering into your hands with a soft but steady contact.
3. Relaxed shoulders, elbows and wrist joints which ensure that your body movements are not transmitted into your hands (so that your hands are completely independent of your seat).

Through experience and training, you will become able to monitor automatically different horses' movements and degrees of bounciness, and adapt your seat accordingly. This is the secret of successful show jumping.

The adaptations which produce the forward forms of seat bring into action different muscles than are used for dressage, so you have to get fit and train in these seats. This is especially true of the light seat, in which you must be able to hold your weight off the horse's back when going cross-country. If you are unfit, you will eventually drop your weight onto the horse's back, becoming an unstable burden.

CHAPTER

15

LISTENING LEGS

A common fault is that riders wanting 'dressage' often attempt to ride 'that style' by lengthening their stirrups by four notches. Wrong! The rider must earn the long stirrups gradually as he stretches his muscles and sinews: his legs 'get longer' from the hip to the heel and necessitate the lengthening stirrups one hole at a time as this development takes place.

Charles de Kunffy

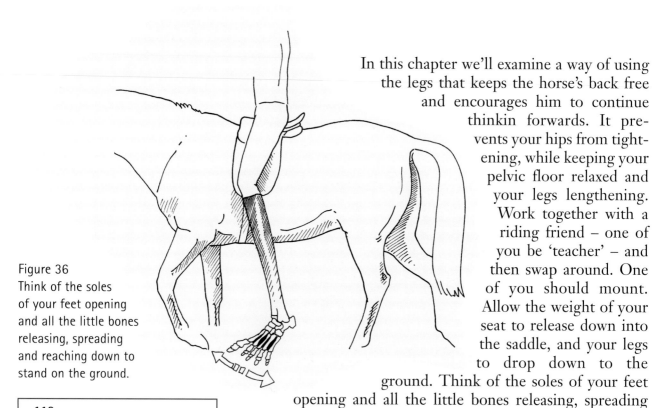

Figure 36
Think of the soles of your feet opening and all the little bones releasing, spreading and reaching down to stand on the ground.

In this chapter we'll examine a way of using the legs that keeps the horse's back free and encourages him to continue thinkin forwards. It prevents your hips from tightening, while keeping your pelvic floor relaxed and your legs lengthening. Work together with a riding friend – one of you be 'teacher' – and then swap around. One of you should mount. Allow the weight of your seat to release down into the saddle, and your legs to drop down to the ground. Think of the soles of your feet opening and all the little bones releasing, spreading and reaching down to stand on the ground (Figure 36).

The following instructions are for the 'teacher'.

1. At halt, check that the rider is sitting centrally in the saddle and adjust as necessary.

2. Place your hand, palm facing upward, under the rider's inside thigh a little way above the knee (as far as you can without strain). This will vary depending on the rider's flexibility (see Photo 30). Then place the other hand on the top of the thigh directly above the first. Think of your arms softening and your hands melting through the rider's leg towards each other; maintain awareness of your surroundings. After a few minutes you should start to feel some release and lengthening of the leg out of the hip joint.

3. When this happens, gently lift the thigh sideways an inch or so away from the saddle (Photo 31). Hold the weight of the leg for a few moments so that the rider can let go even more, then place it back down on the support of the saddle. Repeat step 1. Let the saddle support all the weight of the leg and your hand.

Photo 30

Photo 31

Photo 30–32
Releasing and lengthening the leg.

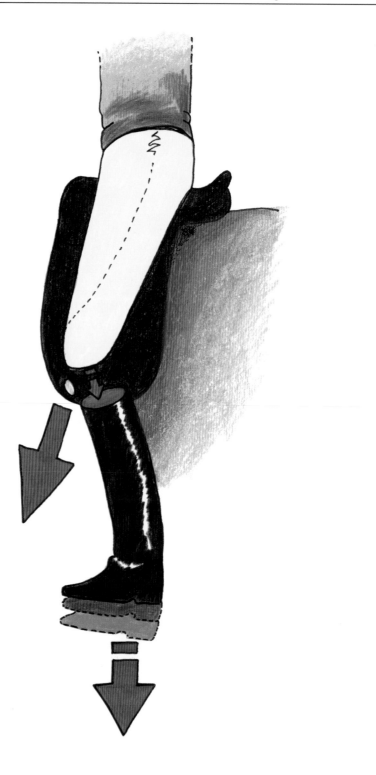

Figure 37
Think of the kneecap releasing
and the whole of the lower leg
hanging down.

4. Now lift the thigh off and gently and gradually spiral it inwards and backwards as much as it will go comfortably without stiffness or strain (Photo 32). Eventually, the thigh will be in a more vertical position. As the leg gets heavier it is releasing more and more out of the hip joint and lower back, becoming more malleable. There should be no stiffness or strain; if there is the rider needs more time on steps 1–3. During this exercise the rider will probably experience internal stretching, which is not to be confused with tension.

5. Place one hand on the rider's lower back (make sure it is not hollowing) and keep the other under the inside thigh.

6. Compare the position of this leg to the other.

7. Repeat with the other leg.

8. Did you notice whether one leg was tighter against the saddle than the other? If, for example, the left was tighter, ask the rider to sit fractionally more to the left and repeat the steps on that leg. Then ask the rider to ride away and check from behind to make sure that they are sitting square over the horse's back as he moves away.

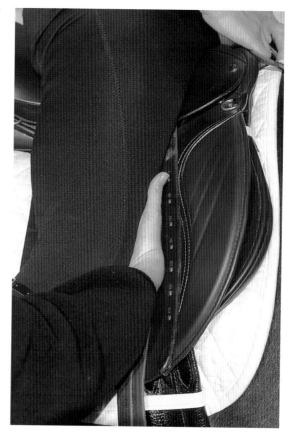

Photo 32

9. Ask the rider to think of their kneecaps releasing and the whole of their legs hanging down (Figure 37). When in motion, the rider should allow the horse's rib-cage to lift them out sideways as well as up and down as it swings from side to side (Figure 38).

10. Now, whilst in motion, ask the rider to lift one leg off and back away from the saddle.

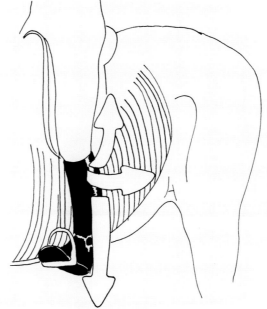

Figure 38
When in motion, allow the horse's rib-cage to lift your legs out sideways as well as up and down.

Figure 39   Wrap your lower leg around the horse's belly by sending your knee vertically down to the ground.

These next steps are for the rider:

11. Wrap your lower leg around the horse's lower belly under the heave line by sending your knee vertically down to the ground (Figure 39). The more you send your knee in this direction the more you will increase the lever action of the lower leg. Keep stretching your calf and heel down so the calf muscles don't become flaccid, while 'scooping up' the horse's belly with your lower leg. In this way the lower leg activates the horse's abdominal muscles, raising his back. You are changing the whole structure of your legs during this exercise, so don't rush – it takes time. Because we are training muscles to take up a position that is unnatural for them it will feel strange and exaggerated, but as your pelvic floor and hips eventually open more you will be suppling up more until, eventually, you will be able to keep your thighs back and down and your lower legs underneath them in contact with the horse's belly.

12. Press your feet back and down onto your stirrups to make sure you are stretching your calf muscles. This strengthens your lower leg.

13. Practise asking the horse to walk on by activating his abdominal muscles with your lower leg. 'Scoop' the horse's belly up into your seat: as soon as he responds stop and let your legs hang and relax. You must not unconsciously nag the horse with your legs every stride as he will switch off and stop listening to them. This habit can be so ingrained that riders don't realise they are doing it.

A useful exercise is to make transitions with your eyes closed, so that you have an opportunity to become conscious of the procedure, and develop conscious feel. Make transitions from halt to walk, and experiment with the placing of your lower leg on different parts of the horse's rib-cage to see which part activates a reflex response which gives a slight lift to his rib-cage as he moves off. The more he has been driven with the seat, the harder it will be for him to lift his rib-cage, because it will be dropped and stiff. The same applies to an ill-fitting saddle: both cause the horse to drop his back.

14. If the horse doesn't respond when you use the lower leg scooping action, first check that you have him on a long rein and that you are not pulling back with your hands. Second, use your whip gently on his shoulder to encourage him to listen more. Remember this is all new to him and, more than likely, he is waiting for you to push with your seat – or whatever you were doing before. Don't worry if he goes slowly at first. He needs to learn to walk on his own without being continually pushed. The horse should do the work; the rider should direct him. If you don't hassle him, after a little while he will develop the confidence to carry you freely forward with a relaxed back.

As soon as the horse moves, relax your legs and open up your awareness to all the space around you: be clear on where you want to go. This process can be repeated in trot, using the exercise explained in the next chapter.

Questionnaire

(Only answer once for each question in this and all following questionnaires.)

1. Did you find it easier to point one knee further down to the ground than the other? If so, which one? (a) left ❑, (b) right ❑, (c) both easily pointed down ❑.
   Score: (a) 1, (b) 1, (c) 3.
2. During this exercise where was your attention? (a) in the past ❑, (b) in the present ❑, (c) in the future ❑.
   Score: (a) 0, (b) 3, (c) 0.
3. How did you keep your seat? (a) passive ❑? (b) driving ❑? (c) did you notice if one seat bone moved less than the other ❑?
   Score: (a) 3, (b) 0, (c) 2.
4. When you placed your legs back and underneath you more (a) did you take your thighs off the saddle ❑? (b) did one thigh move back more easily than the other ❑? (c) did you just bend your lower leg back without moving the thigh ❑? (d) did both thighs move well back and underneath you ❑?
   Score: (a) 2, (b) 1, (c) 0, (d) 3.

5. In trot, how did you press your feet back and down onto the stirrup treads? (a) left more ❑, (b) right more ❑, (c) both together and equal ❑.
   Score: (a) 1, (b) 1, (c) 3.

6. As the horse walked along, did you allow your legs to just hang down and listen to the swing of his rib-cage? (a) right only ❑, (b) left only ❑, (c) both listening together ❑.
   Score: (a) 1, (b) 1, (c) 3.

7. Did you listen to his footfalls and notice when each foot came to the ground (a) sometimes but not very often ❑? (b) never ❑? (c) most of the time ❑?
   Score: (a) 1, (b) 0, (c) 3.

8. How does the horse's back feel under your seat? (a) strong and up with lots of movement ❑, (b) hollow as though you are dropping down a hole ❑, (c) not much movement ❑.
   Score: (a) 3, (b) 0, (c) 0.

9. Does your breathing alter when you use your leg aid? (a) no ❑, (b) sometimes ❑, (c) I hold my breath ❑.
   Score: (a) 3, (b) 1, (c) 0.

10. When you ask the horse to go forwards into walk what happens to the balance of your spine? (Ask your friend to watch and give you feedback until you both agree.) (a) falls back ❑, (b) falls forward ❑, (c) keeps in movement with the horse ❑.
    Score: (a) 0, (b) 0, (c) 3.

11. When you use the leg aids (a) did you lift your ankles up ❑? (b) did you lift one ankle up ❑? (c) did you keep the heels down and calves stretching in both legs evenly ❑?
    Score: (a) 0, (b) 1, (c) 3.

12. Did you press back and down onto the stirrups and think of all the bones in your feet releasing and the arches release as though the soles were gently smiling? (a) I remembered to press both feet down but forgot to allow the arches to release and the toes to spread ❑; (b) I achieved it all with one foot but couldn't get my other foot to have a sense of smiling ❑, (c) I achieved it evenly with both feet ❑.
    Score: (a) 1, (b) 2, (c) 3.

13. When the horse responded to your aid to walk forwards did you (a) relax both legs together ❏? (b) forget to release your right leg ❏? (c) forget to release either leg ❏? (Check whether your friend agrees.)
Score: (a) 3, (b) 1, (c) 0.

14. When you asked your horse to walk forwards from halt practising your new leg aid did you notice (a) a subtle reflex action in his body that lifted his back ❏, (b) he didn't move; I forgot to think forwards to where I wanted to go ❏, (c) he didn't respond so I used my lower legs with a scooping action, backed up with the whip gently on his shoulder, and he responded beautifully ❏.
Score: (a) 3, (b) 0, (c) 3.

15. In transitions, can you keep your spine balanced over the horse's spine (a) without tightening your neck ❏, (b) without tightening his neck ❏, (c) not at all ❏.
Score: (a) 3, (b) 3, (c) 0.

When you have scored 45 points in this questionnaire, you are ready to move on to the next chapter.

BUILDING CONTACT

A horse must be allowed the freedom to carry his neck according to the dictates of the engagement of his haunches. That is the meaning of self-carriage and it must be based on utter freedom from restrictive rein contact. The rider must never seek more contact than the horse does. The bit belongs to the horse!

Charles de Kunffy

All animals, man included – if he is using himself well – work as a whole and follow head-to-tail direction (see Chapter 3 The Primary Freedom). Young babies, for example, have very little head control, yet this is always the first to be established before control of the spine and limbs – then the child walks. However, despite this primary role of the head, it is fundamentally important to remember that it is part of the whole mechanism, none of which can be dealt with in isolation. Therefore, good contact cannot describe only the rider's hands: it describes the delicate interchange of signals between back, hands, legs and seat, monitored by an alert mind. To achieve the contact described by Charles de Kunffy demands great skill and sensitivity, and much practice.

Photo 33
Young child establishing head control.

Fear and Co-contraction

For most actions, there are groups of muscles working in tandem: agonists and their opposing antagonists. When the agonists contract, the antagonists must relax, or the action cannot take place. For example, when you flex your elbows the biceps have to contract while the triceps relax.

In co-contraction, opposing muscle groups contract simultaneously. Make a fist and notice how all the muscles in your forearm contract. The horse often goes into co-contraction as a protection against loss of balance – and so do you!

The horse's neck, like ours, is his main balancing mechanism and acts automatically. So, for example, if the rider has switched off, aimlessly 'mind-hopping', the horse feels confused by the rider's lack of direction, and the rider's wishy-washy attitude

Figure 40
Establishing self-carriage: it must be based on utter freedom from restrictive rein contact.

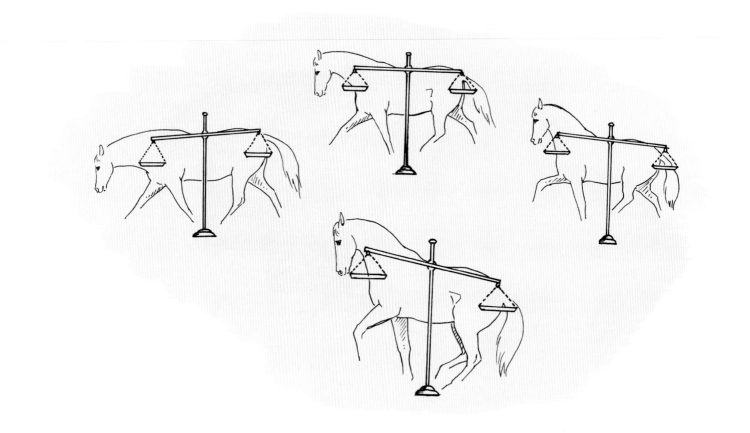

will be reflected in the horse's performance. If the horse is not directed or prepared clearly through bends, circles and transitions, he can't help but lose his balance and co-contract, further upsetting his delicate balancing mechanism. The muscles in his neck come into action to prevent him from losing his balance and falling. He then becomes hard in the hand and set in the neck, so here is a signal from him. What's happening in you – could you be 'mind-hopping'? It is time to tune your brain back in and stop interfering with the good use of your own and your horse's body!

Insecurity causes fear, and frightened horses can't perform to their optimum because of co-contraction. Tension in the body is a symptom of tension in the mind and it is a result of reaction to exterior stimuli. Frightened horses make mistakes and are dangerous to ride. For instance, approaching a fence in blind panic makes the take-off a hit-or-miss affair, and makes a fall much more likely. Frightened horses also run away from the leg, so how can you train such a horse, since training can only begin once he accepts your leg. Frightened horses cannot concentrate; they lose balance and run, blocking communication through the bit.

When horse and rider are tuned into each other harmoniously fear dissipates, necks free, and bodies float, rendering the partnership ready to move in any direction at any moment at the slightest suggestion from the rider. So let's see what we can do about it.

'From Front to Back': a Warning

Charles De Kunffy writes: 'If you work a horse the wrong way, you will ruin him. You will make him a prematurely aged, stiff, broken-down, unhappy creature, full of pain.' He further comments on the dangerous repercussions of forcing your horse into a shape, which is so prevalent in training today:

The horse stiffens and pulls in an effort to save his hocks from the whiplash that results from the tug of war in front. It is hurting him!

If you participate in this pulling contest, the horse comes down so hard on his joints and kicks the ground with so much defiant force as he fights the tortuous pain in his mouth and neck that he eventually breaks down either one or both hocks, depending on single or two-handed pulling by the rider.

Attempting to get the horse on the bit from the front to the back is not only dangerous to the horse's well-being but actively encourages insensitive, back-pulling hands. It doesn't do the rider's back and neck any favours, either. If you recognise yourself in this mode, let go; releasing yourself will release your horse. By now, you will be coming aware of your responsibility as a caretaker carry this knowledge forwards and use it to help yourself and others. Horses, being herd animals, always look for a leader and are usually prepared to forgive and submit to a rider should he deserve that honour – a lesson I think we humans could learn from!

Contact: a Combination of Three Factors

Always remember that contact is not just your hands, but a combination of legs, hand and seat. Through our hands we communicate our intentions to the horse, directing his head and neck and, to some extent, the movement of his hindquarters. Our legs and seat contact are more in charge of the movement of his shoulders, ribs and quarters. At this point we will look more deeply into how the seat, hand and leg combinations work together, and how to check their effectiveness.

The rider's hands, elbows and shoulders should be relaxed but 'alive', ready to respond, act or yield to the horse's mouth at any given moment. It is generally very poor instruction to tell a rider to keep their hands still, except, for example, if the rider is lifting them up and down, pulling them back or using them roughly, upsetting the horse. It is more useful to ask the rider what they are doing with their hands, bringing it into their conscious awareness, letting them tell you.

Riders often stiffen their arms, co-contracting the muscles and creating cast-iron limbs, and telling them to keep their hands still often reinforces this error. More useful phrases for the trainer are:

- Release the front of the shoulders. Allow your shoulder to rest squarely on the top of your rib-cage.
- Lengthen down the back and front of your upper arms so that your elbows can hang down by your sides.
- Allow your elbows to hang down from your shoulders so that they can move forwards and backwards naturally, absorbing the movement of the horse's head and neck as they travel forwards and backwards.

It is important that the rider's biceps remain relaxed so that the elbow can open and close with the movement of the horse's head and neck. The easiest way to become aware of this opening and closing of the elbow is in rising trot. Gently rest your knuckles on either side of the horse's neck, near the wither, resting your thumbs on the horse's crest. This position is useful to bring forward riders who have a tendency to sit or ride behind the movement. It also prevents backward-pulling hands, giving the rider a new feeling and sense of contact, without co-contraction. In this position, watch the front angle of your elbows open and close as you rise and sit to the trot. Be careful not to rotate your wrist inward too much because this gives a backward pull on the rein and leads to flapping elbows. Be careful not to *grip* the reins; gently mould into them, as though you were holding in your hands a little creature that you don't want to crush. All muscles for finger flexion and extension are situated in the forearm. Contraction of these muscles leads to stiff elbows. Any tension in the palm of the hand will cause tension in the horse's mouth. In order to protect himself, the horse will create evasions such as spooking or fixing his eyes on something, thereby putting himself above the bit and out of your control. He will pull against bad hands – wouldn't you? Or he may go behind the bit, or run away hollowing – all of which render communication non-existent.

Exercise: stroking the reins

Stroking the reins (Photo 34 and 35) is the perfect way to develop a sensitive contact with your horse because it keeps your hands moving gently, guarding against gripping or pulling back. It is a brilliant way of retraining a horse who is frightened of the bit, or a young horse who is shy of it.

Only with a sensitive, feather-light contact can the horse hear what you are explaining through your hands and you, in turn, can feel the nuances of balance or resistance in him and act appropriately with your legs and seat. Most horses need a long, light rein contact until they relax and develop confidence in the controller at the other end of the lump of metal in their mouth.

Photo 34–35
Stroking the reins.

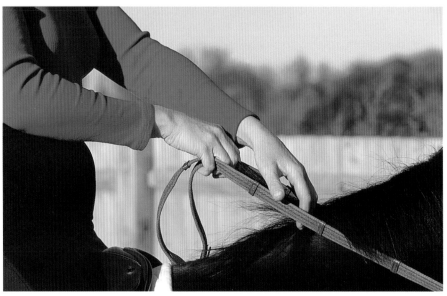

Imagine the reins are silk, and can break easily. Your stroking must be incredibly smooth rather than sticky. You'll know when it's right because you will begin to feel the horse put more pressure on the rein and lengthen his head and neck away from you. If he is frightened or resentful of the bit because he had been the victim of rough hands he may snatch the rein down towards the ground at first. That's great, let the reins slip – he is breaking through his feeling of resentment and fear and at the same time strengthening his back, especially the area where you are sitting. Given time, as his fear subsides, he will relax and go happily long and low.

For those of you who have critics telling you that by doing this exercise you are allowing your horse to drop on his forehand refer them to *The Principles of Riding Book 1* (The Official Instruction Handbook Of The German National Equestrian Federation) pages 160–2, 'Losgelassenheit' and 'Contact'. It summarises: '*Losgelassenheit* is achieved if the young horse moves naturally and rhythmically forward in all three paces, with his neck lowered forwards/downwards and with his back swinging'. It also makes some important points about balance and contact.

When confidence develops into relaxation and primary freedom your horse will naturally take the bit forwards, giving you a more positive, forward-thinking contact – so when he offers it don't spoil it by pulling back and jamming up his body! Watch out for the signals: a heavy, dull contact is usually a sign of a tense mind, jaw, neck, spine and lack of engagement – so check yourself and, like the great masters, let the horse be your teacher!

Exercise: chair work
Use the following exercise to help you develop more sensitivity and independence of the use of your hands in relation to the rest of your body. I find it an excellent way of helping riders to develop this mastery without having to worry about the horse. Later on, when mounted, riders have much more awareness and sensitivity which allows them to work their hands independently of their body.

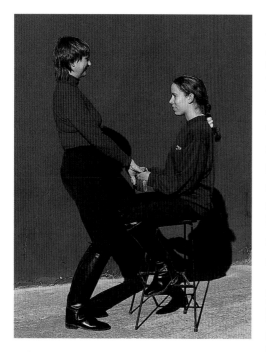

Photo 36

Hold the back of a chair with your fingers spread as in the photo, then go down into a slight squat. What happened to the palms of your hands – did they grip a little? Be aware of your hands on the chair and of any co-contraction. Simulate an *incorrect* rising trot, going up and down vertically (Photo 36). Then simulate a correct rising trot, taking your hips forward and up to meet the chair (Photo 37). Proceed to squat again, then rise and this time ask a friend to place an index finger between your hands and the chair. Now practise the squatting and rising and ask for feedback (Photo 38). Did you grip or pull back? When you are able to rise up and down correctly to different depths, add turns. Can you do these without disturbing your palms?

Rest the chair on its back legs in such a way that it remains balanced. Allow it to fall back and then push it forwards into balance again. When the horse is not taking the bit forwards he will feel like the chair when it has fallen back towards you. In this case you would stretch up through your upper body, stretch your knees and thighs down and keep your calves and heels stretched down while you scoop the horse's belly up with your lower legs. As he stretches forward you will feel more pressure on the reins. If he doesn't offer this then the stroking exercise just described is the best way to encourage him to take the bit forward.

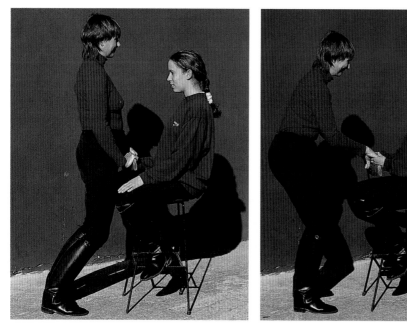

Photo 37

Photo 38

Exercise: straight from the horse's mouth

Reflect on being the horse on the other end of your rein: what would you do if a rider was holding you too tightly – escape the pain in your mouth. On the other hand, if the contact was non-existent, you wouldn't feel or know what to do. To find out for yourself before you ride, play at being horses with your friend: one of you wears the bridle and takes the role of the horse, the other is the rider (see Photos 39 and 40). Close your eyes to let your awareness go deeper. Give each other feedback as you make turns, halts and follow their lead. The one in the horse role can tell the other if one hand is persistently stronger. Watch out for that dreaded right hand. Also, the 'horse' should note how the rider is sitting. On the turns make sure both of you are 'side-by side' (see Chapter 13 Comparing Parts). There is so much you can come up with, so use your creativity and make up your own experiments – it's amazing what you will find. Is the rider gripping at the elbow instead of softening and allowing you to move them? Is the rider tipping to the inside on turns, opening the inside rein too much?

Photo 39–40
Play at being horses.

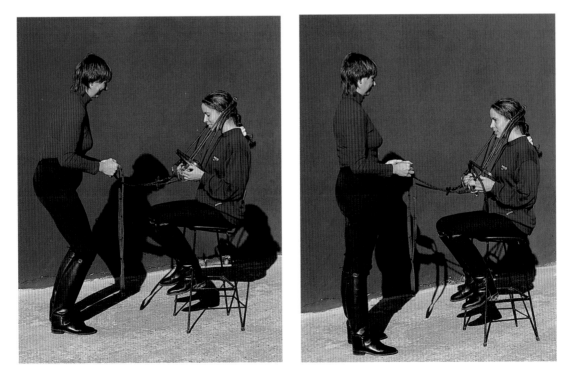

Exercise: observing contact from the ground
If possible, before riding, put a friend on board and watch. How much rein does your horse need in order to stretch his neck forwards and away out of his shoulders in an arc (Figure 41)? Imagine a steady stream of energy flowing, like water, up and over his crest (Figure 42). Is there any point in his neck that is being blocked, causing a flood or bulge in the neck before it flows in between his ears, down his face and onto the ground?

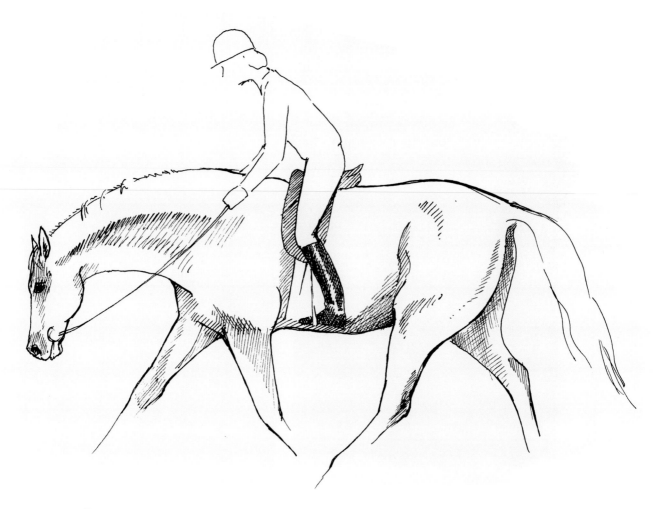

Figure 41   How much rein does your horse need to stretch his neck forwards and away out of his shoulders in an arc?

Figure 42   Imagine a steady stream of energy flowing, like water, up and over the horse's crest.

Figure 43
When he is stretching to his full
extent he will look as though he
is shovelling the arena surface
along with his nose.

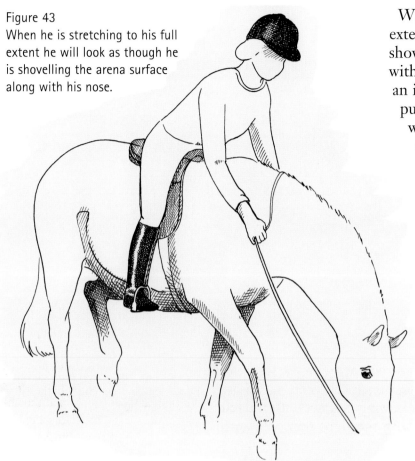

When he is stretching to his full extent he will look as though he is shovelling the arena surface along with his nose (Figure 43). To give you an idea of just how long his spine is, put a pole on the ground. As he walks over the pole, give him a completely loose rein and see how far his neck can stretch. Place your hands forwards as much as possible holding the buckle end of the reins up his crest towards his ears.

Exercise: observing contact mounted; taking up a sensitive contact Let your hands lightly follow the backward and forward movement of the horse's head. Look up his crest and make sure it is long and flowing rather than bulging and flooding back at you.

Take up the reins with your index fingers and thumbs. Let them mould softly into the reins, and feel the horse's mouth. Keep contact with the soft, fleshy parts on the inside of your horse's lips. Feel them through the reins.

Allow the horse to move the whole of your arms from the centre of your spine. Keep your shoulders, elbows and wrists relaxed and following. Then take a normal hand contact.

Stroke his neck, first on one side, then the other (see Figure 44). This will encourage him to stretch his neck more. We want to help him to lengthen and widen his back. Experiment with the position of your spine on his – go into a forward seat. Where do you need to position your upper body to produce more lengthening in the horse?

Figure 44
Stroking the horse's
neck to observe
contact mounted.

Stroke the left side of his neck. This should encourage him to relax his neck muscles. Keep a following contact with the right rein, then take up a delicate, sensitive contact with the left rein; a contact that *doesn't shorten or tighten his neck*! Then stroke the right side of his neck, keeping a following contact with the left rein, and again take up a contact with the right rein. This will help you to find out whether your contact is blocking or following: ask your friend for feedback as to whether you have 25 per cent, 50 per cent, 75 per cent or 100 per cent stretch in the horse. Think of lights like car headlights beaming out of your fingers and thumbs forwards to the horse's mouth (Figure 45).

It is correct theory *when the horse is fully on the aids* to keep the hands still. However, in the early stages of training – stretching – I find there is misinterpretation by teachers who do not understand the biomechanics of the horse. You don't have to take my word for this – watch Reiner Klimke's riders on video – they always warm up on a loose rein, their arms and hands moving literally feet, to allow the horse to stretch his spine fully. A good role model is increasingly difficult to find these days so I recommend you treat yourself to one of Kalman de Jurenak's videos: these provide the best role model I have seen on the market.

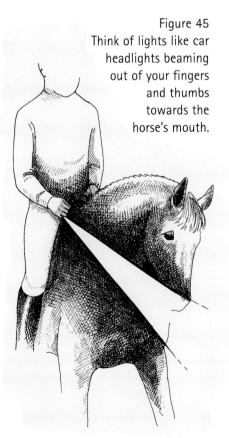

Figure 45
Think of lights like car
headlights beaming
out of your fingers
and thumbs
towards the
horse's mouth.

Questionnaire

When it's safe to do so, close your eyes for a second. Now take your attention to your breathing. Open your eyes.

1. Are your hands pulling backwards on the reins? (a) the right one is ❑, (b) both are ❑, (c) the left one is ❑, (d) both of them are moving forwards with the horse as he stretches his neck away from me ❑.
   Score: (a) 1, (b) 0, (c) 1, (d) 3.

2. Are you aware of your horse's breathing? (a) yes ❑, (b) no ❑, (c) very occasionally ❑.
   Score: (a) 3, (b) 0, (c) 1.

3. When you have your hands on the back of the chair while you are squatting and then standing, are your hands remaining (a) both relaxed ❑, (b) the right one keeps tightening❑, (c) they are both tightening ❑.
   Score: (a) 3, (b) 1, (c) 0.

4. Is your horse's neck (a) arching up and away from you ❑? (b) hollowing ❑? (c) scrunching back and up to you ❑?
   Score: (a) 3, (b) 0, (c) 0.

5. As you are riding along, is the horse (a) behind the bit, feeling like the chair in the exercise when it was falling towards you ❑? (b) taking no contact : rein loose ❑? (c) giving you a feeling of contact and mouthing the bit as when the chair was balanced ❑?
   Score: (a) 0, (b) 0, (c) 3.

6. Is one of your hands being moved more than the other? (a) left is ❑, (b) right is ❑, (c) both are moving forward equally ❑.
   Score: (a) 1, (b) 1, (c) 3.

7. Are you allowing your hands to be moved by the horse's head, or are you blocking (a) at both elbows ❑? (b) in your biceps ❑? (c) in your wrists ❑? (d) both hands are moving freely without restricting the horse's head movement ❑.
   Score: (a) 0, (b) 0, (c) 0, (d) 3.

8. Is his neck stretching now, like the horse in Figure 44? (a) no ❑, (b) only half as much ❑, (c) yes ❑.
   Score: (a) 0, (b) 2, (c) 3.

9. How does the horse respond when you stroke his neck on the left side? (a) he stretches ❑, (b) he does nothing ❑,

(c) he takes the right rein forwards and down ❑.
Score: (a) 3, (b) 0, (c) 3.

10. How does the horse respond when you stroke his neck on the right side? (a) he stretches more than when I stroke the left side ❑, (b) he stretches the left side of his neck more ❑, (c) he doesn't stretch at all ❑.
Score: (a) 2, (b) 3, (c) 0.

11. How much more freedom can you allow in your right arm and hand to achieve more stretch in the horse? (a) a lot ❑, (b) a little more ❑, (c) I am at full freedom ❑.
Score: (a) 1, (b) 2, (c) 3.

12. How much more freedom can you allow in your left arm and hand to achieve more stretch? (a) a lot ❑, (b) a little more ❑, (c) I am at full freedom ❑.
Score: (a) 1, (b) 2, (c) 3.

13. Is your left wrist free and relaxed? (a) yes ❑, (b) no ❑, (c) sometimes ❑.
Score: (a) 3, (b) 0, (c) 1.

14. Is your right wrist free and relaxed? (a) yes ❑, (b) no ❑, (c) sometimes ❑.
Score: (a) 3, (b) 0, (c) 1.

15. Can you imagine each knuckle on your right hand beaming like car headlights forwards to your horse's mouth? (a) some of them ❑, (b) none of them ❑, (c) all of them ❑.
Score: (a) 2, (b) 0, (c) 3.

16. Can you imagine each knuckle on your left hand beaming like car headlights forwards to your horse's mouth? (a) some of them ❑, (b) none of them ❑, (c) all of them ❑.
Score: (a) 2, (b) 0, (c) 3.

17. Are you aware of an opposing stretch dividing your body at the waist area? (a) I can't release my lower body down and around the horse ❑, (b) it's easy for me to release my lower body down and around the horse ❑, (c) it's easier for me to allow my upper body to grow up, forwards and out multi-dimensionally ❑, (d) yes, I can grow up and down evenly ❑.
Score: (a) 0, (b) 1, (c) 2, (d) 3.

18. Is it easy for you to direct your upper body back and up (this doesn't mean *leaning back*) while your elbows hinge

and release as your hands beam forwards and down towards the horse's mouth? (a) no I can't do it, my hands come back with me ❏, (b) I can direct my body back and up but one hand comes back with me ❏, (c) yes, I can go back and up away from the horse's mouth while my hands move into the opposite direction towards his mouth and my elbows hinge and release ❏.
Score: (a) 0, (b) 1, (c) 3.

19. Are you including your legs and seat as part of your contact? (a) yes, I have a good even connection between all three elements ❏, (b) I am including my legs and they are scooping the horse's belly up evenly but I find it hard to co-ordinate with my hands ❏, (c) I notice my right hand and right leg aid is stronger than the left leg and hand ❏.
Score: (a) 3, (b) 2, (c) 1.

20. Is the horse stretching into your hand contact happily whilst mouthing the bit? (a) he's mouthing the bit but doesn't want to take my right hand contact ❏, (b) yes I have a good sub-contact and he's mouthing the bit ❏, (c) his mouth is dry and he's not seeking the contact or paying any attention to my hands ❏.
Score: (a) 2, (b) 3, (c) 0.

When you have scored 60 points in this questionnaire, you are ready to move on to the next chapter.

Body Workshop: Improving Your Feel in Walk

The   art of riding is a celebration of motion, of nature's
rhythms. . . . The rider must live and work in the present, always
grounded in the here and now.

Paul Belasik

The lessons in this chapter are designed to train your body
rhythms to harmonise with those of your horse, keeping your
mind in the present while absorbing and directing the movements of walk.

An independent seat moves in harmony with the horse, while
at the same time the rider is able to give the aids with sensitivity, accuracy and good timing. They are applied at the correct
spot and with the correct pressure, without disturbing the
horse's movement. This will only happen if the rider has the
ability to feel and follow every movement of the horse's back; if
there is no hanging on by the reins; no restriction of the horse's
head, neck and back or gripping with the seat bones, knees or
thighs. In all paces the rider's hands should be totally independent of the horse's movement, never dancing or yanking the
horse in the mouth because of some unexpected movement or
through loss of temper (end-gaining)!

Exercises in Walk

Walk is a four-time gait and now you will learn how to tune into
its rhythm, regulate it and feel the placement of the horse's four
legs working underneath you.

When you give 100 percent your mind becomes quiet.

Four exercises to improve your seat

1. While walking your horse on a long rein ask a friend to lead you. Sense the points of contact of your body on the saddle; pelvic floor, thighs, tail bone. Take a deep breath in through your nose, imagine you have been holding yourself up off the horse and as you exhale let yourself go. Release yourself more into the upward support of the horse; keep your upper body releasing up to avoid slouching. Feel and allow the movements of the horse's back to ripple up and oscillate your tail bone, your 'seat feet' (the bases of your seat bones, which are sitting on either side of his spine), your lower back, pelvis, upper back, and the mid-point in your head. Notice whether your 'seat feet' are evenly supporting the weight above them right up through either side of your torso. Notice whether one seat bone is being moved more than the other. If this is so, move your whole body further over to the side that is moving less, because you may be sitting too far to one side. Ask your friend to check your straightness from behind. Be prepared for it to feel wrong as discussed in Chapter 4 Does Right Feel Right? Any crookedness will feel right because that is what you are used to: moving into straightness usually feels wrong. Knowing this, be prepared to adjust your position on the horse's back, experiencing and meeting parts of your body that you were previously unfamiliar with.

2. Lift your arms up into the air. Allow your body to sink into the upward support of the horse. Stretch right up through your finger tips, pointing them skyward, palms facing inward, little fingers rotated slightly in advance of your thumb. Really 'go for it': *streeeeeeeeeeeeeetch* to your optimum. Success comes through total commitment, not from being wishy-washy – what you focus your attention on grows stronger in your life. As you are stretching to your limit, gently ensure that you are not blocking the free oscillation of your spine at the mid-point in your head: are you freely poised 'on the bit' with your 'crocodile tail' hanging downwards.

3. Allow your upper body (excluding head) to hang from your fingertips onto your 'seat feet', which are standing on either

side of the horse's spine. Keep the 50:50 relationship of the opposing stretch. Use the Darth Vader breathing technique (Chapter 9) to increase your stretch. Divide at the waist: use the breathing to release your upper body up and out of your pelvis. Fill your lower body with breath and breathe through it down to the ground, more, and more, and even more, until you have reached your optimum opposing stretch. Now notice the movement of the horse and allow it to ripple through every cell of your body.

4. Finish by returning your arms to a normal riding position *without collapsing your rib-cage*. Keep open, with your attention expanded more and more up and out into the world by closing those blinds on the back of your eyeballs until you are so present that you are unaware of your body; you are free and open to the sounds, aromas and sensations around you. Enjoy the freedom of self-carriage in motion.

Exercise in feeling your horse

Can you feel the horse's rib-cage swing from side to side as he brings one hind leg stepping under, then the other. This barrel of ribs you are sitting on is like a cradle rocking from side to side. As his rib-cage swings to the right your left 'seat foot' and leg will drop down. Lift your arm up again and notice how, as the 'seat foot' on the left side drops, you absorb the lowering of the horse's back through your own rib-cage as it stretches. Repeat on the other side. Allow your rib-cage to swell and have more space in between each rib, first with your arm lifted, and then in a normal riding position. Keep your ribs open.

The 'seat feet' rise and fall in accord with the movement of the horse's back. As you practise the exercises in this book, you will find that the movement outside your body will gradually become more still, while the movement inside your body will increase as your improved primary control strengthens all the muscles in and around each oscillating vertebra, giving more firmness to the spine. As discussed in Chapter 13 the seat moves on three planes: up/down; back/forward; out to the sides. Cup your 'seat feet' with your hands and feel them move on all three planes. Sideways movements are often neglected in training, leading to a driving seat, stunting the horse's movement and swing. If you have diffi-culty feeling the sideways movement close your eyes and remem-ber that you are on a barrel of ribs that swings from side to side – this usually does the trick.

Exercise in developing rhythm

Let's analyse how you feel the four-beat gait of walk.

Beat 1: when you feel the horse lift your left seat bone up and out, you have felt the first step in the walk sequence.
Beat 2: the left seat bone slides forward and down as your horse's left forefoot engages.
Beat 3: your right seat bone is lifted up and out.
Beat 4: as the horse's right foreleg engages, your right seat bone slides forwards.

First work only on feeling beat 1: when that's clear, add beat 3. Congratulations, you have now felt the hind legs pushing off. When you are accurate and familiar with these beats add the forelegs sequence, beats 2 and 4 to your awareness. Make it into a game with your friend until you can tell at any point where the horse's legs are by the position of your seat bones.

Exercise in altering the length of the stride

As the horse lifts your left and right seat bones, lift and tone them *alternately*. Avoid pinching the seat bones together, because this asks the horse to stop. Practise the following floor exercise until you are aware of the difference. Place the palms of your hands in between your shoulder blades, elbows verti-cally up, armpits open. Now begin floor-walking ('bum-walk-ing'): *streeeeeeeeetch* your elbows up and walk, working the movement through your whole side and out of the top of your elbows (see Photos 41 and 42). Make sure that you stretch the front of your body. Use this exercise to develop more aware-ness of how your seat bones work uni-laterally (alternately). The floor-walking exercise both strengthens and lightens your seat: with practice your back will become more upright as you lengthen through your front. By sending your seat bones fur-ther up into your body, you attract your horse's back up to meet them. His spine will adjust to yours depending on the

Photo 41–42
Floor-walking exercise.

amount of tone you use. More tone means shorter, more collected strides; less tone, more travel allows the stride to lengthen. Try collected work, medium and extended paces as you practise on the the floor. Then work with this whilst riding and experience the law of cause and effect. (Your seat bones should be dancing up and off the saddle – not tight or bearing down. Cup your seat bones with your hands to register the difference in your mind. When it is right, it will feel comfortable for your hands.)

Exercise in working the legs and seat bones independently
While the horse lifts your left seat bone, take your left thigh and knee off and back, away from the saddle and then allow your left leg to rest and hang down heavily while your body is stretching up. Notice that when your seat bone is lifted by the horse your knee has the potential to drop down, bringing the thigh to a more vertical position. Repeat with the right leg.

Riding along, notice how the seat bones work independently of the legs, allowing the thighs to remain more vertical so that when your seat bone lifts, your leg and knee don't have to. Do your 'seat feet' feel as though they are walking on the horse's back? Are your legs further back, draped down and around the horse? The more movement in the horse's back the more you will have to allow your legs to hang down and your seat bones to travel upwards and forwards (remember the image of the watermills in Chapter 13).

Halts and Half-halts

To stop the horse, you first have to stop yourself. Tone your seat bones together until you rise up a little while dropping your legs down and stretching up through your upper body. Tell yourself to be still, and stop. Use your voice and, if necessary, the rein if the horse doesn't get the message.

Fine-tune your seat by cupping your 'seat feet' with the palms of your hands. This will help you to understand their role as checkers and regulators, to become more familiar with what your seat is asking the horse, and will also aid your accuracy. Check that your seat bones tone evenly, because one is usually lazier than the other. The motions of nature's rhymes are very easy to pick up if we take the time to listen to them! So work with the horse, listening and feeling constantly.

If your horse is safe enough, ride the above exercise bareback to develop more rapport and feel between you both. Check the straightness of your seat by using his spine as a guide (see Figure 46). You'll learn more about the way his back works and moves and responds to your new aids. If he responds with tension, your aids are too strong and you are not working with him.

Exercise: riding in the movement
Refresh your memory of the spine oscillation exercise in Chapter 13 so you remember to use it during the following exercises.

A good way to test if you are in the movement is to make a transition from halt to walk. Transitions show up two main

> The motions of nature's rhythm are very easy to pick up if we take the time to listen to them! So work with the horse, listening and feeling constantly.

Figure 46   Check the straightness of your seat by using the horse's spine as a guide.

Figure 47   Falling forwards or backwards during transitions.

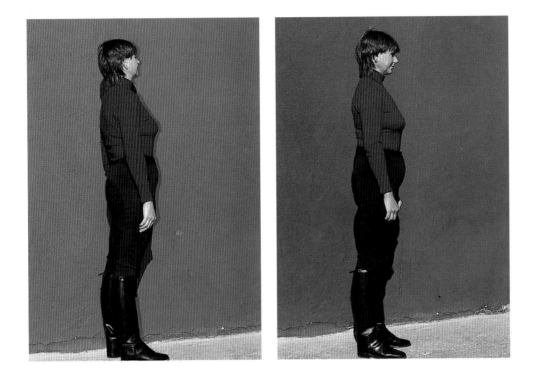

Photo 43–44
Lynn's stance (43)
habitually;
(44) after correction.

faults: falling forwards into the horse's neck or, more commonly, falling backwards (Figure 47). This falling backwards has a lot to do with how we are in life – holding back. Look at Photos 43 and 44. The first shows how Lynn stands habitually, hips forward counter-balanced by shoulders leaning back. This is a recipe for a bad back. Photo 44 shows her after I helped her to release the fix in her mind and body and stop holding back. She is now ready to go at any time – forwards.

In dealing with the first problem of falling forwards most riders are helped by the following images.

1. Hold out your hands in front of you, thumbs uppermost, palms facing each other shoulder distance apart. Imagine you are patting a big ball of air in tiny movements. Can you feel the pressure of the air between your hands? It's like when you try to push two repelling magnets together (see Figure 48a). Now think of a similar ball of air between your spine and the horse's cervical spine (the part in his neck). It's as though your spine and the horse's neck are two repelling

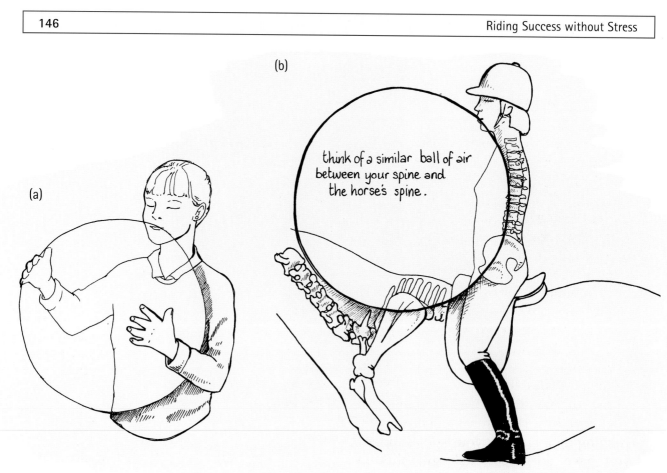

(b)

think of a similar ball of air between your spine and the horse's spine.

(a)

Figure 48
The 'ball of air' image:
(a) Feeling the air pressure between your hands
(b) The ball of air between your spine and the horse's cervical spine.

magnets. You can use his neck as a support to keep your body in balance and away from his neck (Figure 48b).

2. Ask a friend to hold your horse. Close your eyes. Be aware of your spine. Keeping your eyes closed, ask your friend to walk the horse forward a few strides. Halt again. What happened to the balance of your spine when the horse walked on? Did you fall back? Or tip forwards? Or did your spine remain balanced and poised, absorbing the horse's movement? Repeat the exercise, but don't try to think through it. Trust your body's intelligence to keep you in balance with the horse's movement. Attention and practice will get you there. If, however, you keep falling back, you are not forward enough in your thinking. Open your eyes, look at something in the distance, free yourself up and go for it, without closing down your peripheral vision.

Improving Riding Posture

1. Sit with your weight balanced on the central, lowest part of your seat bones, so that you are balanced between the ball and the heel of your 'seat feet'. Make sure you are not sitting on your fork or your tail as this will give you back problems.

2. Think of allowing your ribs to hang down, and your spine to hang down from the crown of your head, which is moving upwards. Think of your neck as light and empty. Take your attention to your feet and think of them releasing from your head as it moves forwards and up; allow the soles of your feet to drop down more into the space below them.

3. To help you achieve a good natural posture that will prevent you from slouching, think of having a big smile across you chest (Figure 49). If you are a chest-lifter – jamming your shoulder-blades together like a sergeant-major – a good image for you to work with is to imagine that you have a continuous stream of tinkling energy running up and down your spine, and that you have developed fish gill slits in between the ribs at the back of your lower rib-cage. Imagine you are breathing in through these instead of through your nose: this image helps to lengthen and widen your back.

Notice how taking your attention to your breathing settles you down and makes you more centred. Take a deep natural breath in through your nose and, as you exhale, relax your whole body, without slouching. Let the horse support your weight, and feel all the sensations in your body, then allow your head and your attention to float up and out into the world.

4. Visit a registered Alexander teacher.

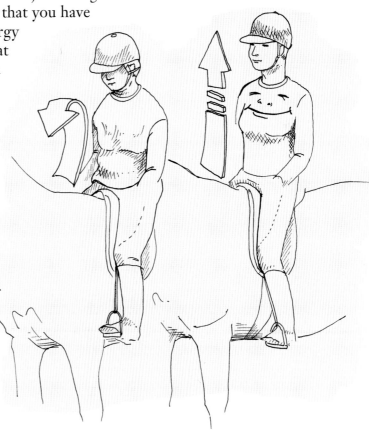

Figure 49
To help you achieve a good natural posture, think of having a big smile across your chest.

Questionnaire

Twenty questions to see if you are celebrating the motions of nature's rhythms.

1. Which way is your right seat bone being moved by the horse? (Then ask yourself the same with the left.) (a) up-down ❏, (b) back-forwards ❏, (c) sideways ❏, (d) all three ways ❏.
   Score: (a) 1, (b) 1, (c) 1, (d) 3.
2. Are you pushing with your seat, blocking out your communication bridge (the horse's middle back) between you and the horse? (a) yes ❏, (b) no ❏.
   Score: (a) 0, (b) 3.

(Stopping driving will, at first, frustrate you because the horse may slow down or even stop purely out of habit. If he stops, just tap him gently on the shoulder with the whip – not to punish but to motivate him. Punishment activates fear reflexes, causing tightening and shortening. Click your tongue or talk to him to give him more encouragement. Eventually, he'll stop waiting for you to push him and gain the confidence to go forwards willingly. Invite his back to come up into your seat by releasing and widening it; grow taller – make sure your thighs are vertical and your knees are deep. He will raise his back up to you and flex his spine. This, in turn, will strengthen his spine for future work in collection.)

3. Take your attention to your seat bones; think of them as little 'seat feet' supporting your upper body. If you are sitting centrally over your horse's back you will have one 'seat foot' on each side of his spine. Where are they in relation to his spine (Figure 47, p143)? Are your 'seat feet' sitting (a) one each side of his spine ❏? (b) to the left of centre ❏? (c) to the right of centre ❏?
   Score: (a) 3, (b) 1, (c) 1.
4. Are you holding yourself up off your horse's back? (a) yes ❏, (b) no ❏.
   Score: (a) 0, (b) 3.

Take a deep breath in through your nose and then let yourself go.

5. Can you feel the movement of the horse's skin moving you around, and the warmth of his body? (a) yes ❏, (b) no ❏.
Score: (a) 3, (b) 0.

6. Are you aware of your own and your horse's breathing patterns? (a) yes ❏, (b) no ❏, (c) sometimes ❏.
Score: (a) 3, (b) 0, (c) 1.

7. Have you got more weight on one seat bone than the other? (a) more weight to the left ❏, (b) more weight to the right ❏, (c) equal ❏.
Score: (a) 1, (b) 1, (c) 3.

8. Is one seat bone more raised up than the other? (a) left is more raised ❏, (b) right is more raised ❏, (c) no, they are equal ❏.
Score: (a) 1, (b) 1, (c) 3.

9. How does the left side of your horse's back feel compared to the right? (a) higher ❏, (b) lower ❏, (c) even ❏.
Score: (a) 1, (b) 1, (c) 3.

10. Does his rib-cage swing more to one side than to the other? (a) more to the right ❏, (b) more to the left ❏, (c) no, they are equal ❏.
Score: (a) 1, (b) 1, (c) 3.

11. When his rib-cage swings to the right, what happens to your left seat bone and leg (a) it lifts ❏, (b) it drops ❏, (c) it doesn't move ❏.
Score: (a) 1, (b) 3, (c) 0.

12. Can you imagine your hips drifting away from each other sideways, far into the fields? (a) I can imagine the right hip drifting ❏, (b) I can imagine the left hip drifting ❏, (c) I can imagine both drifting at the same time ❏.
Score: (a) 1, (b) 1, (c) 3.

13. Are your legs and knees hanging down heavily to the ground?
(a) the right one is ❏, (b) the left one is ❏, (c) both are ❏.
Score: (a) 1, (b) 1, (c) 3.

14. Does your friend agree that you are really letting the horse move your legs/seat/hands? (a) yes ❏, (b) no ❏.
Score: (a) 3, (b) 0.

15. Are you letting your horse move your hands via the reins?
    (a) the right hand ❑, (b) the left hand ❑, (c) both hands ❑.
    Score: (a) 1, (b) 1, (c) 3.

16. Are you allowing your horse to stretch his neck forwards
    and away down to the ground as in Figure 44, (p132)? (a)
    yes ❑, (b) no ❑, (c) a little ❑.
    Score: (a) 3, (b) 0, (c) 1.

17. Is this encouraging him to continually lengthen himself and
    reach forward into the bit with a long, supple spine? (a) yes
    ❑, (b) no ❑.
    Score: (a) 3, (b) 0.

18. Does his barrel of ribs feel more expanded as he stretches
    more, and has his breathing become more efficient? (a) yes
    ❑, (b) no ❑, (c) a little ❑.
    Score: (a) 3, (b) 0, (c) 1.

Widening your attention span.

19. Choose an object you like and look at it as if for the first
    time. Do you see (a) only the shape ❑? (b) both the shape
    and the texture ❑? (c) do you notice three things; shape,
    texture and colour ❑?
    Score: (a) 1, (b) 2, (c) 3.

20. How many sounds can you hear around you? (a) 5 ❑, (b) 10
    ❑, (c) 20 ❑, (d) more ❑.
    Score: (a) 1, (b) 2, (c) 3, (d) 3.

This questionnaire is designed to heighten and open up your
awareness. The more open and alive we are living in the world,
the more our body opens up, maximising its potential. The
more we narrow down our awareness and withdraw from the
world, the more our spine shortens and our body slumps. So it's
your choice! If you scored 60 you are ready to move on to the
next chapter. If you scored below that you need more time and
practice.

RISING TROT

The refinement of the short gait causes Nature to slumber, and obedience becomes unfocused, languid and slow, qualities far removed from the brilliance which is the chief ornament of a well-trained horse.

It is by the trot, the most natural gait, that a horse is rendered light to the hand without ruining its mouth, and quickens the limbs without straining them; for in this movement, which is the highest of the natural gaits, the horse's body is supported by two legs, one fore and one hind; which gives the two others ease in being raised, supported, and extended forward, and hence imparts a high degree of suppleness to all parts of the body.

The trot is hence, without any question, the basis of all lessons designed to render a horse adept and obedient.

de la Guérinière

The working trot is the basic gait in which we develop not only the horse's athletic ability, but also the rider's. By activating the 'hindquarters' of the rider, we increase their self-carriage and strength, enabling them to work both themselves and the horse steadily 'on the bit'.

In the following pages we will be looking at developing impulsion and balance, without the dreaded co-contraction, leading to regular and unconstrained movement. Until a rider can maintain independent, athletic balance and rhythm, their rising trot training will be wishy-washy, lacking the athleticism needed to make it brilliant.

Many students attending my workshops are greatly surprised at the amount of athleticism (under their skin) needed to rise to the trot, freely in the movement. Discovering how ineffective

Figure 50   Riding with the handbrake on.

they have been previously, they practise with enthusiasm – finding it challenging, but fun.

The main obstacles for the rider to overcome are:

1. Not going forwards; keeping the handbrake on; holding back from the space in front of them; loitering behind the movement; rising up vertically rather than forwards and up with an opposing stretch (growing up and down).
2. Knees rising up because the rider's hips don't open at the front angle.
3. Levering themselves up with the reins.
4. Sitting to one side of the horse, weighting one stirrup more than the other (like the hiker, see Figure 23, p88).
5. Twisting.

A good, effective, rising trot demands a great deal of freeing up of both mind and body; going forwards; letting go; horse and rider flowing into the space in front of them. Thanks to the rising trot my students begin to realise just how much opening and freeing is needed to improve the horse's movement. With this mental attitude established, the body structuring can then proceed.

For people living sedentary lives the following exercises are not so easy, because we spend so much of our time sitting, usually slouched, under-using our bodies. This has the effect of weakening and closing down the front of the body, which then requires quite a lot of work to get it moving. The following exercises may feel very awkward and unclassical at first, so remember that you are working on the means whereby, not the end-gain. Beware of end-gaining well-wishers advising you that your lower leg is far too far back, that you are moving around too much or that you must have a line shoulder, hip, heel, as they are working in the conventional way – ends justifying the means. Remember the lady with the leg of lamb suffering from archaic parent conditioning (Chapter 5): your well-wishing friends will be suffering from archaic teacher conditioning. Unaware of biomechanics, they are 'following the ideal,' instead of 'getting real'. (See where that got me in Chapter 10). The whole psychology behind this is fear of failure: 'I must get it right' in order not to appear as if I don't know. But, daring to

Figure 51
The key points of rising trot.

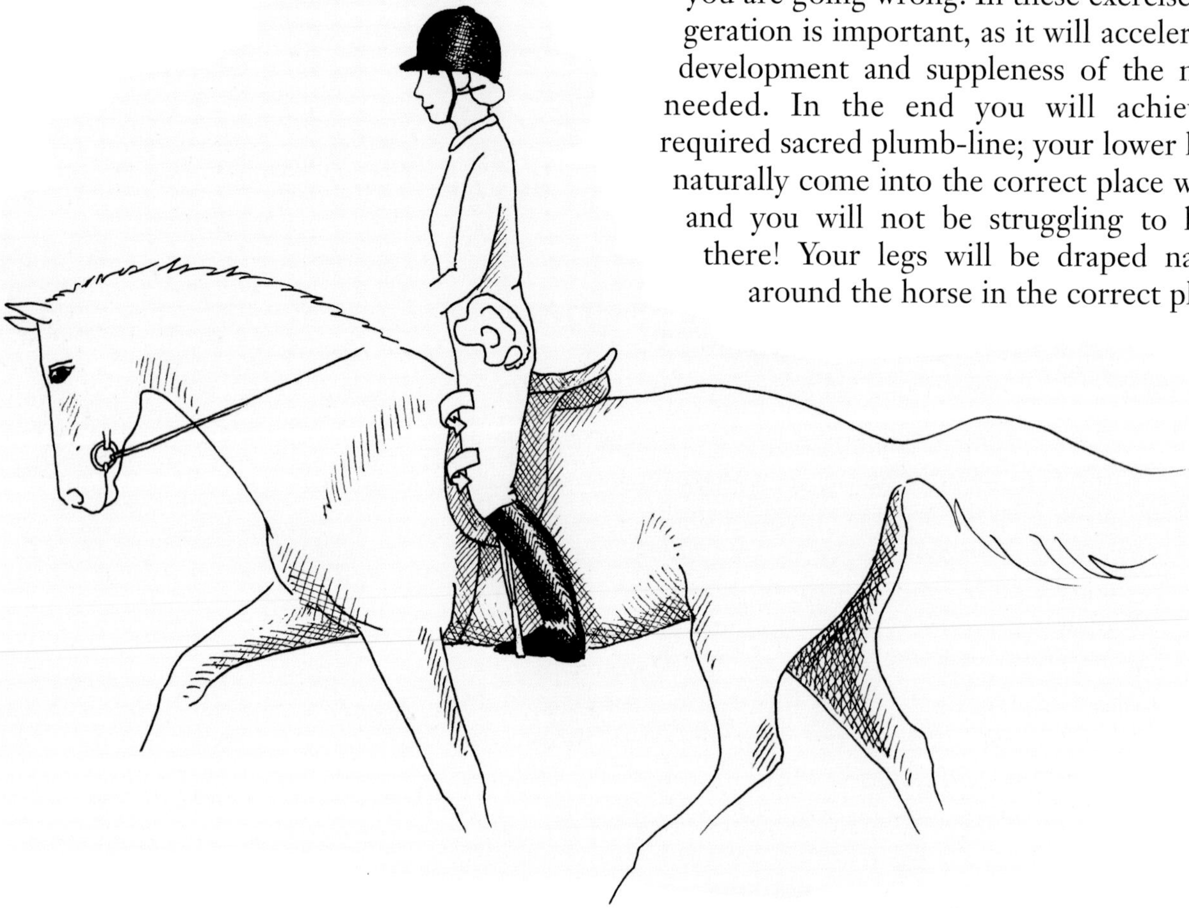

fail is your biggest stepping-stone to success because you are beginning to know where you are going wrong. In these exercises exaggeration is important, as it will accelerate the development and suppleness of the muscles needed. In the end you will achieve the required sacred plumb-line; your lower leg will naturally come into the correct place with eas and you will not be struggling to keep it there! Your legs will be draped naturally around the horse in the correct place.

Here are six pointers to achieving a good, travelling rising trot.

1. Thigh rolls gently inward.
2. Heel rolls away and directs down to horse's hind foot so that the whole leg slips down the horse's side.
3. Seat bones forwards and up. To achieve this the pelvis has to swing forwards and upwards, sending your seat bones in an upward direction toward the horse's ears.
4. Knees deep; your knees drop forwards and down into the knee rolls. Think of kneeling down.

5. Nose down. Your attention and head lead the movement in a forwards and upward direction, into the space above and in front of you. You allow your spine to follow, and your nose to drop. Allow your back to widen into the space behind you.

6. Elbows bent softly, embracing your rib-cage while your shoulder blades slide down over the ribs to meet your hips.

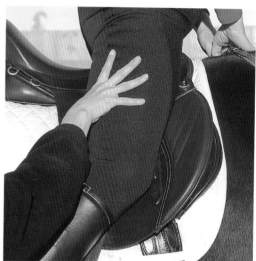

Photo 45

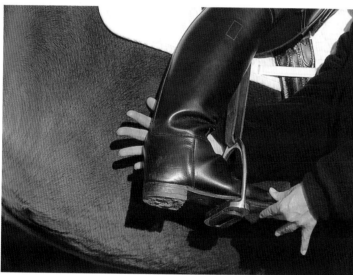

Photo 46

Photo 47

Photo 45–47 Working towards correct rising trot. Photo 45: Step one, thigh roll. Photo 46: Heel away. Here, Lynne's ankles are a little stiff. They will release with Alexander lessons, as was the case with the author's own. Photo 47: Although Lynne's upper body is in alignment, she needs Alexander lessons to create more length between her shoulder-blades and tail-bone because her pelvis is tipping forwards. The shortening and narrowing of her lower back is a result of how she stands and uses herself in everyday life. As her head, neck and back release so will her legs, giving her a deeper seat which will balance the tipping of her pelvis.

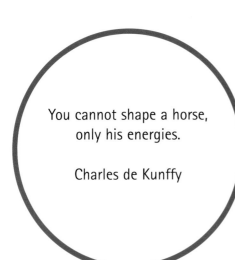

You cannot shape a horse,
only his energies.

Charles de Kunffy

Stationary Exercises

First practise rising trot whilst stationary. Ask a friend to assist you. Use a neck strap to grab hold of in case you lose your balance and fall backwards.

1. Stand up in your stirrups, then place yourself over the left stirrup and walk your right leg back and underneath you – then do the same with the left. Make sure you walk your knees back under your hips so that your feet are angled in the direction of the horse's hind feet. You may be surprised how far back your lower leg and feet are placed in order to get your thigh vertical – every rider is different – but make sure you keep the angle at the back of your knee open by stretching down through your calf and heel.

2. Thigh roll gives you the required muscle tone with an open pelvic floor, and depth of seat to keep you in the movement. (Watch that you don't roll your knee in too much, thus bringing your lower leg out.) You must keep your thighs rolled inward when you sit as well as when you rise – this stops you falling behind the movement.

3. Heel away. Allow your lower leg to continue that spiral down to your feet, gently spiralling the heel away from the horse's side. Toes now pointing forwards.

4. Seat bones forwards and up towards the horse's ears. To open up the front angle of the hips in order to send the seat bones forward and up, my students find it very helpful to imagine that someone is throwing a big beach-ball just above their navel and they are gently punching it back to them with their stomach and midriff through the horse's ears. Use this image to help you propel the horse forwards. The longer you want the stride to be, the further you punch the ball away from you, by allowing your pelvis to travel further. The shorter you want the stride to be, the less you punch the ball. So, if you've got a horse who is running away, tone your seat bones together: the punch will then be very small, and deliberately in a slower rhythm than the horse's until the horse comes back to your rhythm and slows down.

You monitor the amount of punch you use in the rising trot according to what the horse is doing and what you require of him. Building athleticism in your own body as above will give you the full range of movement which will enable you to ride any stride, from the most collected to the most extended, without hindering the horse's steps.

Check that you remain 'on the bit': allow yourself to lengthen from your pubic arch to your chin and from your hips to your mastoids (the mastoid is the bone that protrudes behind your ear lobe).

5. Knees deep. Allow your knees to drop down into the knee rolls as you rise. Imagine you are kneeling on the ground. Let your knees slide down the saddle with each rising. 'Beam' your knees down to the ground; allow the front of your hips to open and land on the front of your thighs, kneeling down into the knee rolls, then stretch your lower legs down.

6. 'On the bit'. Your attention and head lead the movement in a forwards and upward direction, into the space above and in front of you. Allow your spine to follow, your nose to drop as you rise, and your back to lengthen and widen into the space behind you. Ask a friend to check that you are 'on the bit' and 'equal on both reins' both as you rise and sit. Allow the support of the stirrups to come up into your feet, sinking your heels down and allowing your toes to spread, rather than pushing up on the stirrups with the balls of your feet, which would raise your heels and cause you to tip forwards. Now allow the support of the stirrups to raise up through your body until you sense them supporting you right up to your head. Check that you are 'on the bit', not pulling your head and neck back and down and going 'above the bit'.

7. Allow your body to suspend down to the ground, developing an opposing stretch. Release the front of the ankle up to the knee and the back of the knee down the calf to the heel and into the ground: allow your feet to lengthen and widen. My students like the image of themselves as a shining star, radiating out brightly into the world to keep themselves open and freeing into the space in front of and around them (see Figure 52). So, keep your legs back and underneath you and

Figure 52   Imagine yourself like a shining star, radiating brightly out into the world.

'shine through' from inside out. Your arms and legs are extensions of the whole of you radiating out into the world.

8. Elbows bent softly, embracing your rib-cage while your shoulder blades slide down over the ribs to meet your hips. Your elbows adjusting their angle, opening and closing naturally as you rise and sit.

Firming and Toning Up Your Position

While rising and sitting at the halt, keep your seat bones toned together, placing your hand under them (Photos 48 and 49). Make sure that, when you fold at the hip to sit, you land lightly as far to the front of the saddle as possible – landing on the cantle tips your pelvis forward and makes it more difficult to rise.

When you are happy with your rising and sitting at the halt, practise in walk, then in trot. If possible, practise the trot first on the lunge on a nice, steady horse. If you get left behind the movement, use your neck strap to prevent banging down on to the

Photo 48–49
Toning the seat bones whilst rising and sitting at the halt.

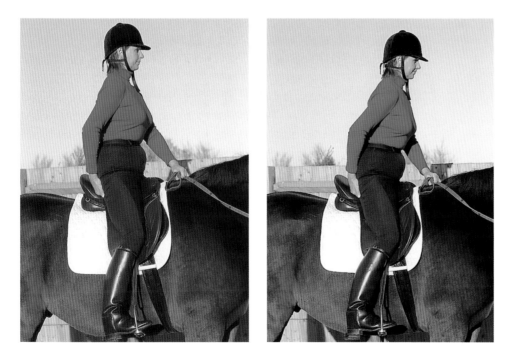

horse's back. Keep freeing yourself up and out into the world until you find a balancing point that keeps your hips open, knees down and lower leg back. Trot slowly and only for a few strides.

You will soon become supple enough to remain open in the front of your body while your legs remain back and underneath you. Alexander lessons are very helpful here for the serious rider. Use the 'ball of air' as an extra aid to keep you opening up in front and imagine you are growing a big, heavy crocodile tail to prevent your pelvis from tipping forwards too much and to keep you lengthening and widening your spine.

The Magical Aids

The big secret to successful riding is to be open and to free up more and more, and the movement doesn't stop. Stop holding back away from the space in front of you which blocks both your forward movement and the horse's. Always allow the vertebrae in the horse's neck to float away from you, otherwise you will scrunch his neck in, preventing his back from raising up and restricting the free forward movement that strengthens his top line.

Strengthening and Testing Your New Position

Look at the trees around you. Think of yourself as a tree. Your waist is the ground line. Free your waist. Feel warm, liquid clay flowing from your waist into the pelvis, down into the hips, down into the horse's body, down into your thighs, knees, lower legs, ankles, feet, and dripping down into the ground.

Free your waist again and let the trunk grow up through the middle of your rib-cage, breastbone and upper back; through your neck into the middle of your skull. Free the midpoint in your head and allow the tree to grow up and out into the space above you. Keep growing out into your environment. Now keep your attention up and out into the world, include in your awareness the soles of your feet; think of them smiling and releasing through the stirrups, down into the core of the earth (see Figure 53).

Allow yourself to feel and permit the movement of the horse's rib-cage as it swings from side to side. Think of your knees as hollow and empty and your kneecaps falling down to the ground, never pinching the horse's sides when you rise. Check that you are not over doing the inward spiral of the thigh and that you are not pulling yourself up on the reins.

How is your contact now? Where is your attention now?

Let's see whether you are now in the movement with the horse. Normally, when you change your diagonal in rising trot, you sit for an extra beat. For this exercise, we'll apply the same principle, but instead of sitting an extra beat, you will stand for an extra beat – two beats in the air. Keep changing the diagonal in the air every few strides and notice what happens to your balance. Did you fall back? Did you tip forwards? Did you land heavily? (Check by placing your hand between your seat and the saddle.) Keep working on this, counting the rhythm of the trot out loud, until you remain poised and in balance. Then increase the length of time you spend in the air until you can balance effortlessly in the movement for at least six strides.

Finally, check whether your diagonals are even. Take your attention to your right hip: is it dropping and releasing away from your left shoulder as you rise and sit? Then take your attention to your left hip. Think of it dropping and drifting away from your right shoulder. Is one diagonal more supple than the other?

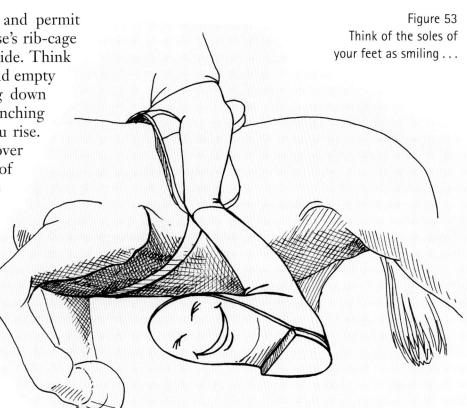

Figure 53
Think of the soles of
your feet as smiling . . .

Questionnaire

1. Did you roll onto the front inside of the thigh when you rose? (a) only on the left leg ❏, (b) only on the right leg ❏, (c) yes, on both legs ❏.
   Score: (a) 1, (b) 1, (c) 3.

2. Did you move your heel away from the horse's side in order to allow your toe to turn to the front? (a) yes, both heels ❏, (b) only the left ❏, (c) only the right ❏.
   Score: (a) 3, (b) 1, (c) 1.

3. Did you move your seat bones forward and up to your horse's ears? (a) yes, to my full capacity and then I could monitor it depending on what length of stride I wanted from the horse ❏, (b) not very much – I found it difficult ❏, (c) no, I rose vertically up in to the air ❏, (d) one seat bone moved more easily than the other ❏.
   Score: (a) 3, (b) 1, (c) 0, (d) 1.

4. Did you drop your nose down a little as you were rising to allow your head to move forwards and up? (a) no I forgot ❏, (b) I thought I did, but my friend said my nose was still pointing up ❏, (c) yes ❏.
   Score: (a) 0, (b) 1, (c) 3.

5. Did your jaw remain relaxed? (a) I don't know ❏, (b) no, it tightened ❏, (c) yes, it stayed relaxed ❏.
   Score: (a) 0, (b) 0, (c) 3.

6. Are you remembering to keep your rib-cage forwards and up, and rolling your thighs forwards when you sit to prevent you from collapsing your lower back? (a) no my rib-cage collapsed down towards my tail bone, so I must have slouched ❏, (b) yes, I kept thinking forwards, up and out with the horse which kept my rib-cage moving in that direction and I am keeping my 'crocodile tail' to prevent my lower back from hollowing v ❏, (c) I don't know ❏.
   Score: (a) 0, (b) 3, (c) 0.

7. Does it help you to deepen your seat if you think of your hips drifting away from each other sideways into the fields while keeping your thighs gently rolled in and sliding downwards? (a) yes ❏, (b) I can't make that image work for me ❏, (c) a little bit ❏.
   Score: (a) 3, (b) 0, (c) 1.

8. Are you remembering to allow your feet to drop and your toes to spread like duck's feet down to the horse's hind feet as you rise

The first energy you produce in the horse should produce his posture. . . and only the surplus energy beyond that can be spent for transportation.

with your heel lower than the ball of your foot? (a) only with my right foot ❑, (b) only with my left foot ❑, (c) I am allowing both feet to move down and spread but I can't release my heels down ❑, (d) yes, both of them are lengthening down to the ground; my heels are dropping and the soles of my feet are smiling (Figure 54) ❑.

8. Score: (a) 1, (b) 1, (c) 2, (d) 3.
9. As you rise do you feel as though you are kneeling down? (a) yes ❑, (b) only with my left knee ❑, (c) only with my right knee ❑, (d) no, my knees are moving upwards ❑.
   Score: (a) 3, (b) 1, (c) 1, (d) 0.
10. Are you falling back when you change the diagonal in the air? (a) yes ❑, (b) sometimes ❑, (c) never ❑.
    Score: (a) 0, (b) 0, (c) 3.
11. Do you fall forwards when you change the diagonal in the air? (a) yes ❑, (b) no ❑, (c) sometimes ❑.
    Score: (a) 0, (b) 3, (c) 1.
12. Do you raise your hands when you rise? (a) yes ❑, (b) no ❑, (c) only my right hand ❑, (d) only my left hand ❑.
    Score: (a) 0, (b) 3, (c) 1, (d) 1.
13. Do you use the reins to help you to balance? (a) never ❑, (b) sometimes ❑, (c) sometimes with my right hand ❑, (d) sometimes with my left hand ❑.
    Score: (a) 3, (b) 0, (c) 0, (d) 0.
14. Can you allow your hips to drop away from the opposite shoulder a little more without raising your shoulder while you are rising and sitting? (a) no ❑, (b) yes, my right hip from my left shoulder ❑, (c) I can't feel the connection from my hips to the opposite shoulder at all ❑, (d) yes, I can release more in both my diagonals ❑.
    Score: (a) 0, (b) 2, (c) 0, (d) 3.
15. When you rise, do you get a feeling of shining like a star (see Figure 53)? (a) yes a little, but my pelvis is tipping forwards ❑, (b) not at all ❑, (c) yes, and I am imagining I have a heavy crocodile tail hanging down to the ground to keep my pelvis level ❑.
    Score: (a) 1, (b) 0, (c) 3.

When you have scored 45 points in this questionnaire, you are ready to move on to the next chapter.

CHAPTER

19

SITTING TROT

There is a saying that the horse should enjoy himself in his work, otherwise neither the rider nor the horse would be able to give an elegant performance.

de Pluvinel

Sitting trot must be built up gradually: balancing in sitting trot is an art, and has many components to it. Start very slowly and increase the pace a little at a time, until you remain centred and move easily with the horse. Trot little and often, mixing sitting with rising. When you are sitting you should remain adhesive to the saddle: if you are going really slowly and you are still leaving the saddle, hold the saddle and lean back until you feel the heels of your 'seat feet', then gradually become vertical.

While sitting to the trot feel the left, right movement of the horse's hips as he brings his hind legs under. Allow your hips to travel left and right in rhythm with the horse's hips so they are moving unilaterally. Notice your inner thighs touching the saddle alternately as the horse lowers and raises his hips. Keep growing up through the front of your upper body and smiling across your chest so that your upper torso supports your elbows and keeps them soft and hanging to absorb the movement between you and the horse's mouth (see Figure 54).

If you are banging about on your horse's back during sitting trot you are going too fast for your own, and your horse's, ability. You are most likely too far forward with your upper body, which will cause you to bounce and grip with your knees. This has the effect of pushing the seat out of the saddle. The rider

Figure 54   The elements of sitting trot – correct.

Figure 55   The elements of sitting trot – incorrect.

then tenses against the discomfort of the movement, causing co-contraction – arms, hands and neck tighten, disrupting the contact with the horse's mouth. The horse responds by hollowing his back, shortening his stride and making it bumpy. The rider loses balance, and the whole thing becomes a mess (see Figure 55).

If the horse's back is dropped or hollow, then in truth you shouldn't be sitting on it, period. I have met many riders who confess that they only sit in trot because they are dressage riders who 'believe' this is correct – a form of misguided snobbery, I think. They are usually driving with the seat; seat bones stuck together sliding forwards and back, rather than separating and moving up and down with the movement of the horse's back, hips and hind feet. Many riders hover above the horse's back in front of the vertical controlling the movements with the rein, thinking they are being kind when, in truth, they are simply ineffective. These riders have only got half the story; they are usually unaware of the correct use of the seat, and they do not sit like Nuno Oliviera or have Iberian horses. They are using the ends to justify the means.

Preparatory Work

If your horse is hollow, then he isn't ready to sit on yet, so work more on riding long and low (see Chapter 16); this will produce more stretch and strength in his back. With his back strengthened in this way you will find his true movement. Every horse has a movement personal to them and if you free them and allow them to move, they will take it up. Interestingly, because the horse's back becomes more engaged as the movement gets bigger, it gives you more support and is stiller, making it easier for you to sit on. The next stage is to elevate your own and the horse's forehand. For this use school movements and transitions to produce more engagement and activity of the quarters, which at the same time lightens the forehand. As you allow the hind legs to lift your 'seat feet' up and down, use the following exercise to help strengthen and support your upper body.

Exercise: stretching to improve posture

Ride on the lunge on a quiet horse. Lift your elbows skyward and place the palms of your hands in between your shoulder-blades. As you breathe in and out, stretch your elbows as high as you can skywards until your upper arms are vertical, opening your armpits wide. This stretches the front of your spine as it lengthens your whole front and sides, and it strengthens your stomach muscles. It also brings your upper body up and out of your pelvis, lightening it. In this way your pelvis is left free to be oscillated by the horse, and the oscillations then ripple further up into your upper body and head. This is posture at its strongest and most elegant.

As you are stretching up, give your seat bones to the horse; allow him to lift and drop them more. Take the whole of both legs off the horse and back. You will probably be bounced more, because you are allowing his back to work more. Take your attention out more and allow yourself to float effortlessly with your horse. Keep your shoulders over your hips to avoid tipping forward, which would only make the bounce worse. Feel proud; use this emotion to improve your carriage and make you 'bigger'; make sure your seat bones are moving unilaterally.

Let your back oscillate gently from your head to your tail as it receives the upward support of the horse. Create more length between your mastoid bones and your hips. 'Give' the weight of your lower body to the horse and allow it to release down and around him. Eventually you will find a place where the skin of your buttocks doesn't leave the saddle – the bounce being absorbed in your spine. Experiment with leaning back and forward and sitting centrally.

Increasing Seat Control and Cadence in Trot

This next technique lifts the horse's back and keeps him 'on your seat' while, at the same time, creating more spring and lift in the stride by toning and releasing the seat bones alternately. Tone the left seat bone as he lifts it and then release it as he drops it (the same applying to the right seat bone. Use the bum-walking technique described in Chapter 17 to get the correct feel. Now you can influence the rhythm and length of stride by controlling the amount of movement of your seat bones and spine. For more engagement, allow your seat bones to dance higher into your body while your legs release down to the ground. Keep your spine more still. For extension, use less tone and allow the seat bones alternately to travel more. Imagine that each hip is a big watermill, paddling and rolling forward with the horse's movement, lengthening the stride. Think of paddling each watermill backward to shorten the stride. (Note: toning your seat bones means that they go up into the body and lighten the seat. They do not clench, push or grind down into the horse's back. Cup your seat bones with your hands and feel the effect. They should tone evenly, but often one seat bone is lazier. In this case bum-walk on the floor until they are even. If your horse hollows or dislikes this technique, either you are overdoing it or you are out of synch with his movement.)

By using this monitoring system you can shorten, lengthen or lift the stride as necessary and keep the horse 'on the seat'. If your horse tends to 'run away' from you (by now, he shouldn't), use half-halts as described in Chapter 17, then take up the rhythm with your seat bones again; think 'passage' as you proudly come up and out into the world. If he continues to run, take rising trot and slow him down with your rise. Whilst practising sitting trot, rise every ten strides to check that you are not making the horse hollow. Support his belly with your lower legs and play with your fingers on the rein – just enough to get his attention, not to haul his head in, or waggle it from side to side!

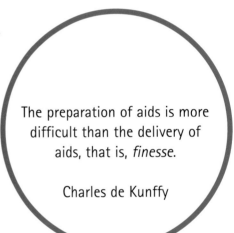

The preparation of aids is more difficult than the delivery of aids, that is, *finesse*.

Charles de Kunffy

Questionnaire

1. While you are sitting to the trot, where is your attention? (a) up and out of my body ❏, (b) I am tightening in and down and so is my attention ❏, (c) I don't know where it is ❏.
   Score: (a) 3, (b) 1 for observation, (c) 0.
2. Are your hips alive and moving up and down alternately with the horse's corresponding hind legs? (a) only the right one is ❏, (b) only the left one is ❏, (c) yes, they are both moving

separately with the horse's corresponding hind legs ❏, (d) I can feel my seat bones, but I can't feel the horse's hind legs pushing them up ❏.
Score: (a) 1, (b) 1, (c) 3, (d) 2.

3. While sitting, are you allowing your seat bones to be lifted in such a way that the front hinges of your hip joints are open to absorb the forward and upward movement of your seat bones? Place your hand there and see: (a) no ❏, (b) only my left hip joint is allowing ❏, (c) only my right one is allowing ❏, (d) yes, both hip joints are opening and closing as the horse lifts my seat bones unilaterally ❏.
Score: (a) 0, (b) 1, (c) 1, (d) 3.

4. Are you remembering to use the ball of air image to help support you as you ease your legs off and back and the bounce increases? (a) yes, and it really helps ❏, (b) no, because I'm frightened of falling backwards ❏, (c) it only works now and again because I keep bouncing forwards ❏.
Score: (a) 3, (b) score 1 for trying and hold the pommel for support, (c) score 2 and hold the pommel and lean back until you remain adhesive to the saddle then gradually come up to the vertical.

5. Is it getting easier to take your legs off and back more in order to allow them to drape down and around the horse's sides to the ground? (a) yes, I'm getting much more supple ❏, (b) no ❏, (c) a little bit ❏.
Score: (a) 3, (b) 0 – you are not working yourself athletically enough bring the whole of the legs off and back, (c) 1.

6. Are you using a forward-working hand? (a) no, I keep forgetting ❏, (b) sometimes I forget and find that my horse's neck is scrunching back towards me ❏, (c) yes ❏.
Score: (a) 0, (b) 1, (c) 3.

7. Is the horse rounded and reaching for the bit with a space under his chin? (This space is very important because it stretches the underside of the horse's spine – similar to the elbow raising exercise in the human – and lengthens it more, allowing even more length in his top line). (a) yes ❏, (b) no ❏, (c) a little more than usual ❏.
Score: (a) 3, (b) 0, (c) 1.

8. Are your seat bones and hips absorbing the sideways swing

of the horse's back? (a) yes, fully ❏, (b) one is but the other is a bit stiff ❏, (c) no, I can't feel it ❏.

Score: (a) 3, (b) 1, (c) score 0 and go back to the walk chapter.

9. While you are practising sitting trot is your horse hollowing? (a) no ❏, (b) yes ❏, (c) a bit ❏.

Score: (a) 3, (b) score 0: go back to rising to raise the horse's back, then practise moving your seat bones alternately in a light seat until you can gradually bring your weight back without hollowing him; check that you are not preventing his neck from lengthening away from you, (c) score 1: scoop up his belly with your lower leg to lift his back, allowing your seat bones to move separately and *keep your attention up and out*.

10. Once your horse remains round and you are absorbing the movement with an adhesive sitting trot, can you influence the size of his stride by the amount of collection and lengthening of your own seat bones and spine (how much you allow them to move)? For collecting the horse you will tone them, making them rise up further into your body; for lengthening him they will be toned but travelling forwards and upwards more. There will also be a greater distance between your mastoid processes and your hips. (a) yes, it works brilliantly: I can see that to create something in the horse I first have to perform it in myself ❏, (b) no, I can't differentiate between up and forwards ❏, (c) it's a bit hit and miss ❏.

Score: (a) 3, (b) score 0: go back to the beginning of chapter 12, (c) 1: you need to practise and to re-read Part Two of this book again.

When you have scored 30 points in this questionnaire, you are ready to move on to the next chapter.

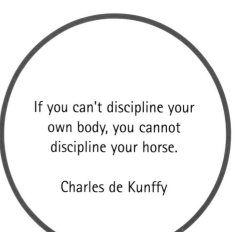

If you can't discipline your own body, you cannot discipline your horse.

Charles de Kunffy

CHAPTER
20

CANTER

Elegance on horseback consists of a straight and free position as a result of a well balanced body; as a result the rider maintains, during all the movements the horse makes, without losing his seat, as much as he is able to, in an appropriate balance, an air of comfort and freedom, which makes him an elegant rider.

de la Guérinière

Canter is the most impulsive of the horse's gaits. During the cycle of the stride, the horse's centre of gravity has to move backwards so that he can lift his forelegs and shoulders into canter (see Figure 56). He must therefore be allowed freedom in his head, neck and back in order for the powerful surge of energy to move through him from his hindquarters to these parts. As he brings his weight back and 'sits', all the joints in his quarters flex, engaging his hind feet further under his body. This sitting action lightens and elevates his forehand and frees his shoulders.

In Chapter 13 we discussed comparing parts and, in canter, you must keep side by side with your horse in order for his foreleg to strike off whilst allowing the outside hind to support. Your outside leg brushes back to announce the canter and, if necessary, to prevent the quarters from swinging out. Check with the inside leg if he tries to bring his quarters in. Place your inside hip forward while your inside leg maintains the powerful surge of energy moving through and out of the poll. If the horse is striking off on the wrong lead, it is usually (saddle problems and injury aside) because he is still not straight, so correct his one-sidedness in walk and trot until he is four-footed, with an inside bend. Note that there is no miracle cure for crookedness in canter; it has to be cured in walk and trot. When the horse gives you a good bend in trot he should strike off effortlessly on the correct canter lead. (When first introducing canter it is best to use a light seat until the horse's back is up and round and he seeks to take the contact to the ground.)

Developing Use of the Horse's Back

To develop the maximum use of the horse's spine in canter I recommend the following procedure.

To start with, lunge the horse without a rider. There are two reasons for this: first, to give him more freedom in the way he uses himself; second, to show you how the canter works biomechanically. When you lunge him, start off on his easy side. Lift the rein as you give the verbal command, 'canter', then press him forward until he canters. Repeat this until he is sharp to the vocal aid. Then use the vocal aid whilst riding and, as you did on the lunge, press him forwards with your lower legs (keeping yourself in a light seat) until he breaks into canter. Retain a light seat throughout this lesson. Ask for canter

Figure 56
The rider's opposing stretch allows the horse freedom in canter.

in a corner and don't worry if he breaks the canter at this stage, because he is learning to balance in a different way, with total freedom. At first, he will more than likely lift his head and neck and canter too fast. If so, stroke his neck and give the outside rein forwards for a few strides, then the inside rein (Figure 44, p133). Support him with your outside leg and rein to steady him a little; play with your fingers on the reins (without shortening his neck) to relax his jaw and keep him listening to you. Make sure you are allowing the outside of *his* body its full stretch by giving the outside of *your* body its full stretch (don't hollow your inside). Then, when he's more steady, push both hands forward up his crest. Allow the horse to jump up in front during the transitions; this will make him lighter and more engaged. If he is allowed to play, he will soon develop the balance and impulsion required to maintain the canter for longer periods. The reason I recommend this procedure is because there is usually so much effort and strain attached to cantering; the rider pushing, grinding and gripping excessively while the instructor bawls 'he must stay in canter' as though it is some cardinal sin for the horse to break into trot in the early stages of training.

If you let him take his nose to the ground (into 'long and low' – Figure 41, p130), going slowly, he will very soon learn to canter rhythmically forward with free, balanced, ground-covering strides, and with an arched carriage of neck and head. If you are too frightened to go forward with him in this way, ask someone to lunge you on a quiet horse in long side reins, allowing the horse to go long and low until you gain the confidence to ride in canter with an allowing hand. Riding in this way will prevent you from pulling back with the rein – a major problem in canter. (Many riders think that keeping the reins short keeps the horse off the forehand, but this is wrong – it just makes him hollow.)

Once an even rhythm is established, use your collecting and extending aids. By using a light seat in canter, keeping your seat bones together you collect; by letting go, you extend. Use half-halts to increase and decrease the length of stride; this will improve balance and engagement. As soon as the horse has discovered how to control his balance he will gain confidence and drop his head and neck, stretching and rounding onto a light contact, which brings his hind legs further underneath him. Once your horse has established a good round, rhythmic, canter you can start to establish your sitting canter.

Rider's Position

In canter it is essential that you allow your 'seat feet' to follow the movement of the horse's back. In order to do this you have to allow the horse to draw your pelvis forwards and backwards, keeping your lower back and your hips free and following. Allow your legs to hang down heavily to the ground. Your buttocks remain gently toned, knees and ankles elastic and rib-cage floating.

In canter, as you can see in Figure 57, the horse's back slants downhill. This is why you must relax and lengthen the front of your body, allowing it to stretch like a rubber band. Give yourself to the horse. Use your 'ball of air' for support; allow your hip joints to open. Open the back of your knees to allow the weight of your legs down to the floor, thus keeping yourself vertical and giving you the feeling of standing on the ground with a horse between your legs. You are now more of thee balls of your 'seat feet'.

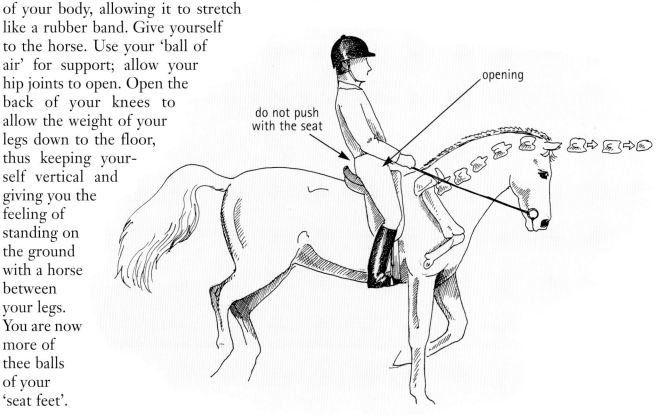

do not push with the seat

opening

Figure 57
The downhill slant of the horse's back during canter.

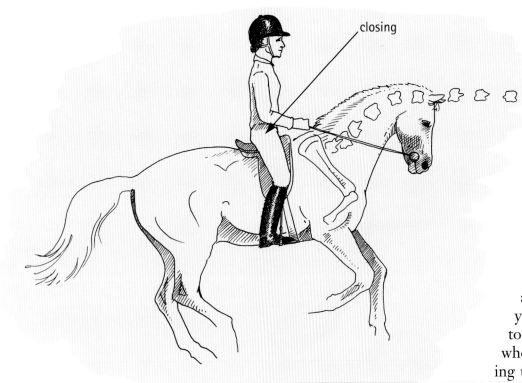

closing

Figure 58
The effect of the horse's movement in canter on the rider's hips and pelvis.

Next, the horse's movement brings you up first to the lowest central part of the ischial bones then to the back edge, when your hip joints will close (Figure 58). Thus the horse's motion should automatically close and open your hips, and move your pelvis. All you have to do is allow this to happen. Feel the front, middle and back of the saddle. If you don't allow the horse to move you in this way when his hind feet are coming under you, you will block his movement, hindering the engagement of his hind-quarters.

Use the 'ball of air' and your breathing to give you more support; breathe in through your nose for five strides while the horse is 'going down'. Notice how this helps you to keep lengthening through your front when the horse drops down away from you. Feel the back, middle and front of your 'seat feet' and allow that 50:50 relationship between the weight of your body and the support of his. Sit, and let the horse do the work. To ask for strike off, place your inside seat bone forwards and support with the inside leg on the girth. Announce the canter with the outside leg sliding back, behind the girth. This automatically turns the hips in the correct direction. Arms, elbows and shoulders hang and 'give' up the crest if the horse is shortening his neck: as the horse goes down the inside hip and leg will be moved forwards automatically as a result of the canter action.

To help develop a long, effective leg in canter take both legs off and back and imagine your feet are broad and long – like the webbed feet of a duck. Imagine that your toes are lengthening and widening; the whole of the soles of your feet spread down onto the stirrups; to the ground.

Exercise: stretching in canter on a long rein

Practise this exercise first on the lunge, on the horse's easy rein. In canter, take your reins into your right hand: put your left hand into the air; fingertips pointing to the sky. As you feel the horse fall away from you towards the ground, breathe in continually and 'hang from your fingertips', allowing your hip joints to open. Receive the upward support from the horse as you give your lower body to that support. Do this for about five strides then, breathing out, keep 'hanging from your fingertips', noticing his body come back up to you. Notice your hip joints closing for five strides, then change hands. Repeat the exercise on the other rein.

Questionnaire

1. Did you relax the front of your body and allow it to stretch like a rubber band? (a) only at the lower abdomen ❏, (b) no, I couldn't allow the front of my body to stretch ❏, (c) yes, I allowed the stretch to go all the way from my pubic arch to my throat ❏.
   Score: (a) 1, (b) 0, (c) 3.

2. Did you give yourself to the horse? (a) no, I'm still gripping my thigh up, jamming and preventing the front angle of my hip joint from opening ❏, (b) I could only allow with my lower body; the stretch needed to give fully to the horse doesn't work through my upper body yet ❏, (c) yes, when the horse dropped away from me on the down beat of the canter I absorbed the drop through my upper body ❏.
   Score: (a) score 1 for observation, (b) 2, (c) 3.

3. Did you use your 'ball of air' for support? (a) yes ❏, (b) sometimes ❏, (c) no, I forgot ❏.
   Score: (a) 3, (b) 2, (c) 0.

4. Did you allow your hip joints to open? (a) yes ❏, (b) no, neither; I'm still gripping up ❏, (c) only one joint will open at the moment ❏.
   Score: (a) 3, (b) 0, (c) 1.

5. Did you release your knee down to the ground to allow the weight of your body to slide down the saddle? (a) yes ❏, (b) no ❏, (c) one knee more than the other ❏.
   Score: (a) 3, (b) 0, (c) 1.

6. Did you get the sensation of standing on the ground with the horse in between your legs when he was balanced in canter? (a) yes ❏, (b) no, my knees still come up ❏, (c) only vaguely ❏.
   Score: (a) 3, (b) 0, (c) 1.

7. Did you feel it when the horse placed you on the front rim of your ischial bones as his forehand dropped away from you? (a) no ❏, (b) yes ❏, (c) sometimes ❏.
   Score: (a) 0, (b) 3, (c) 2.

8. Did you feel it when the horse placed you on the lowest central part of your ischial bones then on the back edge, closing your hips? (a) no ❏, (b) yes clearly ❏, (c) sometimes ❏.
   Score: (a) 0, (b) 3, (c) 2.

9. Did you notice that the horse's motion automatically closed and opened your hips and moved your pelvis? (a) yes ❏, (b) no ❏, (c) sometimes ❏.
   Score: (a) 3, (b) 0, (c) 2.

10. Could you 'allow' it to happen? (a) yes ❏, (b) no ❏, (c) sometimes ❏.
    . Score: (a) 3, (b) 0, (c) 2.

11. When the horse is moving you in canter, are you aware of the front, middle and back of the saddle? (a) yes ❏, (b) sometimes ❏, (c) no ❏.
    . Score: (a) 3, (b) 2, (c) 0.

12. Did you find using the 'ball of air' gave you more support? (a) yes ❏, (b) no ❏, (c) sometimes ❏.
    Score: (a) 3, (b) 0, (c) 2.

13. Did you remember to breathe in through your nose and stretch up, keeping your head and neck forwards and up 'on the bit' when the horse was going down? (a) yes ❏, (b) sometimes ❏, (c) no ❏.
    Score: (a) 3, (b) 3, (c) 0.

14. Did you breathe out when he was coming up, then find a natural breathing pattern of perhaps 'in' for three strides

The job of the hands is to create longitudinal flexion by yielding.

Charles de Kunffy

the 'out' for three strides keeping yourself 'on the bit'? (a) yes ❏, (b) no ❏, (c) sometimes ❏.
Score: (a) 3, (b) 0, (c) 3.

15. Did you feel the back, middle and front of your 'seat feet' and allow that 50:50 relationship between the weight of your body and the support of his? (a) yes ❏, (b) no ❏, (c) sometimes ❏.
Score: (a) 3, (b) 0, (c) 2.

16. Did you relax and let the horse do the work? (a) yes ❏, (b) no ❏, (c) sometimes ❏.
Score: (a) 3, (b) 0, (c) 2.

17. Did the image of duck's webbed feet help you to widen and lengthen your feet, and your feet to spread down onto the stirrups; to the ground? (a) yes ❏, (b) no ❏, (c) sometimes ❏.
Score: (a) 3, (b) 0, (c) 2.

18. When you took the reins into the right hand and put your left hand in the air, fingertips pointing to the sky as you felt the front of the horse fall away from you towards the ground, did you find 'hanging from your fingertips' helped you to receive the upward support from the horse as you gave your lower body to that support? (a) yes ❏, (b) no ❏, (c) sometimes ❏.
Score: (a) 3, (b) 0, (c) 2.

19. Whilst 'hanging from your fingertips', did you notice that the horse's body coming back up to you closed your hip joints? (a) yes ❏, (b) no ❏, (c) sometimes ❏.
Score: (a) 3, (b) 0, (c) 2.

20. Did you keep your attention up, out and lively in the world, including the various parts of yourself you were observing in the big picture, rather than narrowing into yourself, losing awareness of your environment? (a) yes ❏, (b) no, when I thought of each individual part, I completely looked inward, blind to what was going on outside myself ❏, (c) I was totally unaware of where my mind was ❏.
Score: (a) 3, (b) score 2 for observation, (c) 0.

When you have scored 60 points in this questionnaire, you have successfully completed all the exercises in *Riding Success Without Stress Book 1*. Congratulations.

CONCLUSION

Realizing the merits of the equestrian arts, the traditional leading classes of Western society made sure that their young elite received an education on horseback. For horses can educate through first hand, subjective, personal experiences unlike human tutors, teachers and professors can ever do. Horses can build character, not merely urge one to improve on it. Horses forge the mind, the character, the emotions and inner lives of humans. People can talk to one another about all these things and remain distanced and lonesome. In the partnership with a horse, one is seldom lacking for thought, emotion and inspiration. One is always attended by a great companion.

Charles de Kunffy

This quotation sums up so eloquently my feelings on the education a horse has to offer a rider. I hope that this book has helped you to be more process-directed, filled in training gaps, and enlightened you more on how the Alexander technique can be applied to riding in order to give you a firm foundation for a good position.

Throughout the book, rather than throwing a whole bunch of facts at you, I have shared personal recollections to help give you a personal insight of the principles involved. I hope that these have helped you to realise how easy it is to be misled.

I hope you will use the knowledge in this book to help you to stand back and avoid bad teaching methods and social conditioning. You will then be your own person, a conscious choice-maker who can discriminate and choose a wise, skilled teacher. The world of wonderment is far more exciting than the illusionary world of 'playing the game.' You will be free to enjoy the special charm, affection and guidance that your horse has to give to you, as a gift, for your own self-development.

Author's mailing address:

Joni Bentley
c/o J. A. Allen and Co. Ltd.
1 Lower Grosvenor Place
London SW1W OEL

Alexander technique governing bodies:

Alexander Technique International (ATI)
1692 Massachusetts Ave.
3rd Floor
Cambridge
MA02138
USA

(ATI Great Britain
66c Thurlestone Road
London SE17 0PD)

Society of Teachers of the Alexander Technique (STAT)
20 London House
266 Fulham Road
London SW10 9EL

Index

Note: page numbers in *italics* refer to figures and photographs